First Workshop on Economics and Natural Language Processing (ECONLP 2018)

Held at ACL 2018

Melbourne, Australia
20 July 2018

ISBN: 978-1-5108-6718-5

ACL 2018

Economics and Natural Language Processing

Proceedings of the First Workshop (ECONLP 2018)

July 20, 2018
Melbourne, Australia

Introduction

Welcome to ECONLP 2018, the First Workshop on Economics and Natural Language Processing held at ACL 2018 in Melbourne, Australia on July 20, 2018.

This workshop addresses the increasing relevance of natural language processing for regional, national and international economy, both in terms of already launched language technology products and systems, as well as new methodologies and techniques emerging in interaction with the paradigm of computational social science and computational economics. The focus of the workshop is on the many ways how NLP alters business relations and procedures, economic transactions, and the roles of human and computational actors involved in economic activities.

The topics at the intersection of NLP, economy, business, organization, enterprise, management and consumer studies that ECONLP addresses include (the list below is by no means exhaustive):

- NLP-based (stock) *market* analytics, e.g., prediction of economic performance indicators (trend prediction, volatility analysis, performance forecasting, etc.), by analyzing verbal statements of enterprises, businesses, companies, and associated legal or administrative actors

- NLP-based *product* analytics, e.g., based on (social) media monitoring, summarizing reviews, classifying and mining complaint messages, etc.

- NLP-based *customer* analytics, e.g., customer profiling, tracking product/company preferences, screening customer reviews or complaints, identifying high-influentials, etc.

- NLP-based *organization/enterprise* analytics, e.g., by tracing and altering their social images in the media, conducting fraud analysis based on screening business, sustainability and auditing reports

- *Market sentiments and emotions* with evidence collected from consumers, and enterprises, subjective verbal behavior and their communication about products and services

- *Competitive intelligence services* based on NLP tooling

- Relationship and interaction between *quantitative* (structured) economic data (e.g., time series data) and *qualitative* (unstructured verbal) economic data (such as press releases, newswire streams, social media contents, etc.)

- *Information management* based on organizing and archiving continuous verbal streams of communication of organizations and enterprises (emails, meeting minutes, business letters, etc.)

- *Credibility and trust models* of agents in the economic process (e.g., as retailers, shoppers, suppliers, advertisers, market intermediaries) based on text/opinion mining of communication traces and legacy data from past interaction activities

- Verbally fluent *software agents* (language bots) as actors in economic processes who take different roles in the business process and thus embody, e.g., models of persuasion, fair trading and information exchange, or conflicting interests, etc.

- *Enterprise search engines* (e-commerce, e-marketing) — electronic equivalents of yellow pages (e-shops) which inform/consult/guide consumers in the market space based on natural language interaction

- *Consumer search engines*, market monitors, product/service recommender systems that allow consumers to search for products based on verbally expressed individual needs, requirements and constraints, including economic matchmaking functionality

- *Customer-supplier interaction platforms* (e.g., service providing portals and help desks, newsgroups) and transaction support systems based on collaborative natural language communication

- Specialized modes of *information extraction and text mining* in economic domains, e.g., temporal event or transaction mining

- *Information aggregation* from single sources, e.g., review summaries, automatic threading of dialogues, issue or argument tracking in dialogues

- *Economy-specific text genres* (business reports, sustainability reports, auditing documents, product reviews, economic newswire, business letters, legal documents, etc.) and their implications for NLP

- *Corpora and annotations policies* (guidelines, metadata schemata, etc.) for economic NLP

- Dedicated *ontologies* for economics and adaptation of *lexicons* for economic NLP

- Dedicated *software resources* for economic NLP (e.g., NER taggers, sublanguage parsers, pipelines for processing economic discourse)

Two types of papers were solicited for the ECONLP workshop:

- Long papers (8+1 pages) should describe solid results with strong experimental, empirical or theoretical/formal backing,

- Short papers (4+1 pages) should describe work in progress where preliminary results have already been worked out.

We received 16 submissions (from which 2 were withdrawn during the review process), and based a rigorous review process, we accepted 2 as long papers, 7 as short papers and rejected 5 from the remaining 14 papers. Accordingly the acceptance (rejection) rate was 64% (36%). The acceptance/rejection ratio amounts to 1.9.

We want to thank those colleagues who submitted their work to our workshop and hope that their efforts will start a process of sustainable activities in this exciting domain. In particular, we also want to thank our PC members whose thorough and in-time reviews were the basis for properly selecting the papers presented at this workshop. Finally, we hope the attendants of the workshop enjoyed the presentations and discussions in Melbourne.

The organizers of ECONLP 2018

Udo Hahn
Véronique Hoste
Ming-Feng Tsai

Workshop Organizers:

Udo Hahn   Friedrich-Schiller-Universität Jena, Germany (Chairman)
Véronique Hoste   Ghent University, Belgium
Ming-Feng Tsai   National Chengchi University, Taiwan

Program Committee:

Sven Buechel   Friedrich-Schiller-Universität Jena, Germany
Erik Cambria   Nanyang Technological University, Singapore
Philipp Cimiano   Universität Bielefeld, Germany
Xiao Ding   Harbin Institute of Technology, China
Junwen Duan   Harbin Institute of Technology, China
Flavius Frasincar   Erasmus Universiteit Rotterdam, Netherlands
Petr Hájek   Univerzita Pardubice, Czech Republic
Allan Hanbury   Technische Universität Wien, Austria
Pekka Malo   Aalto University, Finland
Viktor Pekar   University of Birmingham, England, U.K.
Paul Rayson   Lancaster University, England, U.K.
Samuel Rönnqvist   University of Turku, Finland
Kiyoaki Shirai   Japan Advanced Institute of Science and Technology (JAIST), Japan
Padmini Srinivasan   University of Iowa, Iowa City, IA, USA
Chuan-Ju Wang   Academia Sinica, Taiwan
Yue Zhang   Singapore University of Technology and Design, Singapore

Table of Contents

Conference Program

July 20, 2018

09:00–09:30	*Introduction to the ECONLP Workshop* Udo Hahn
09:30–10:00	*Economic Event Detection in Company-Specific News Text* Gilles Jacobs, Els Lefever and Véronique Hoste
10:00–10:30	*Causality Analysis of Twitter Sentiments and Stock Market Returns* Narges Tabari, Piyusha Biswas, Bhanu Praneeth, Armin Seyeditabari, Mirsad Hadzikadic and Wlodek Zadrozny
10:30–11:00	***Morning Coffee Break***
11:00–11:20	*A Corpus of Corporate Annual and Social Responsibility Reports: 280 Million Tokens of Balanced Organizational Writing* Sebastian G.M. Händschke, Sven Buechel, Jan Goldenstein, Philipp Poschmann, Tinghui Duan, Peter Walgenbach and Udo Hahn
11:20–11:40	*Word Embeddings-Based Uncertainty Detection in Financial Disclosures* Christoph Kilian Theil, Sanja Štajner and Heiner Stuckenschmidt
11:40–12:00	*A Simple End-to-End Question Answering Model for Product Information* Tuan Lai, Trung Bui, Sheng Li and Nedim Lipka
12:00–14:00	***Lunch Break***
14:00–14:20	*Sentence Classification for Investment Rules Detection* Youness Mansar and Sira Ferradans
14:20–14:40	*Leveraging News Sentiment to Improve Microblog Sentiment Classification in the Financial Domain* Tobias Daudert, Paul Buitelaar and Sapna Negi
14:40–15:00	*Implicit and Explicit Aspect Extraction in Financial Microblogs* Thomas Gaillat, Bernardo Stearns, Gopal Sridhar, Ross McDermott, Manel Zarrouk and Brian Davis
15:00–15:20	*Unsupervised Word Influencer Networks from News Streams* Ananth Balashankar, Sunandan Chakraborty and Lakshminarayanan Subramanian
15:30–16:00	***Afternoon Coffee Break***

16:00–16:30   *Discussion and Wrap-up*

16:30–17:30   Poster Session - All of the Papers Presented at the Workshop

Economic Event Detection in Company-Specific News Text

Gilles Jacobs, Els Lefever and Véronique Hoste

Language and Translation Technology Team, Ghent University

Groot-Brittanniëlaan 45

9000 Ghent, Belgium

`{gillesm.jacobs,els.lefever,veronique.hoste}@ugent.be`

Abstract

This paper presents a dataset and super-vised classification approach for economic event detection in English news articles. Currently, the economic domain is lacking resources and methods for data-driven supervised event detection. The detection task is conceived as a sentence-level classification task for 10 different economic event types. Two different machine learning approaches were tested: a rich feature set Support Vector Machine (SVM) set-up and a word-vector-based long short-term memory recurrent neural network (RNN-LSTM) set-up. We show satisfactory results for most event types, with the linear kernel SVM outperforming the other experimental set-ups.

1 Introduction

In the financial domain, the way companies are perceived by investors is influenced by the news published about those companies (Engle and Ng, 1993; Tetlock, 2007; Mian and Sankaraguruswamy, 2012). Tetlock (2007), for example, tried to characterize the relationship between the content of media reports and daily stock market activity, focusing on the immediate influence of the Wall Street Journal's 'Abreast of the Market' column on U.S. stock market returns. One of his major findings was that high levels of media pessimism robustly predict downward pressure on market prices.

To provide some insights into the way markets react to new information about companies, financial economists have conducted event studies. These event studies measure the impact of a specific event on the value of a firm (MacKinlay, 1997). They offer insight into the extent to which shareholders of acquired firms gain better returns during mergers, or examine the behavior of companies stock prices around events such as dividend announcements or stock splits. Studying the impact of specific events on the stock markets, however, is a labor-intensive process, starting with the identification of a given event, the estimation of abnormal returns to separate the general movement of stock returns from an individual stock return, followed by a number of statistical tests seeking evidence to support the event's economic significance. Since identifying news published about certain events in an automatic way enables researchers in the field of event studies to process more data in less time, and can consequently lead to new insights into the correlation between events and stock market movements, automatic techniques have been proposed to detect economic events in text.

Most of the existing approaches to the detection of economic events, however, are knowledge-based and pattern-based (Arendarenko and Kakkonen, 2012; Hogenboom et al., 2013; Du et al., 2016). These use rule-sets or ontology knowledge-bases which are largely or fully created by hand. The Stock Sonar project (Feldman et al., 2011) notably uses domain experts to formulate event rules for rule-based stock sentiment analysis. This technology has been successfully used in assessing the impact of events on the stock market (Boudoukh et al., 2016) and in formulating trading strategies (Ben Ami and Feldman, 2017). Other approaches conceptualize economic event detection as the extraction of event tuples (Ding et al., 2015) or as semantic frame parsing (Xie et al., 2013).

A drawback of knowledge-based information extraction methods is that creating rules and ontologies is a difficult, time-consuming process. Furthermore, defining a set of strict rules often re-

Proceedings of the First Workshop on Economics and Natural Language Processing, pages 1–10
Melbourne, Australia, July 20, 2018. ©2018 Association for Computational Linguistics

sults in low recall scores, since these rules usually cover only a portion of the many various ways in which certain information can be lexicalized. Thus, the need for flexible data-driven approaches, which do not require predefined ontological resources, arises. Rönnqvist and Sarlin (2017) provide an example of successful data-driven, weakly-supervised distress event detection based on bank entity mentions. Here, bank distress events are conceptualized as mentions of bank entities in a time-window and no typology classification is assigned. We are not aware of any published data-driven, supervised event detection approaches for the economic domain. However, in general domain event extraction, as embodied by projects such as ACE (Ahn, 2006) and ERE/TAC-KBP (Mitamura et al., 2016), supervised methods for extraction of event structures are predominant because of their promise of improved performance.

As discussed in Sprugnoli and Tonelli (2017), the definition of events in the field of information extraction differs widely. In this work, we employ a conceptualization of economic event detection as *retrieving textually reported real-world occurrences, actions, relations, and situations involving companies and firms*. Unlike other supervised data-driven 'event extraction' tasks such as in the ACE/ERE programs (Aguilar et al., 2014), we do not conceptualize events as structured schemata/frames, but more limited as textual mentions of real-world occurrences. The task presented here is often also referred to as event 'mention', 'nugget', or 'trigger' detection. The classification experiments described here are currently at the sentence-level, but our event annotation scheme is token-level.

In this paper, we tackle the task of economic event detection by means of a supervised machine learning approach, which we expect will be able to detect a wider variety of lexicalizations of economic events than pattern-based approaches. We consider economic event detection as a sentence-level multi-label classification task. The goal is to automatically assign the presence of a set of predetermined economic event categories in a sentence of a news article.

In previous work on the Dutch counterpart of this dataset, (Lefever and Hoste, 2016) has shown that SVM classification obtained decent results. Here, we compare two different machine learning approaches, viz. a rich feature set Support Vector Machine (SVM) approach, and a word-vector-based sequence long short-term memory recurrent neural network (RNN-LSTM) approach. We show that supervised classification is a viable approach to extract economic events, with the linear kernel SVM obtaining the best classification performance.

The remainder of this paper is structured as follows. In Section 2, we present the annotated corpus of financial news articles we constructed. Section 3 introduces our two classification approaches to economic event detection, followed by an overview of the results in Section 4. In Section 5, we conduct an error analysis to gain insights in the main shortcomings of the current approach. Section 6 formulates some conclusions and ideas for future work.

2 Data Description

In this section, we describe the SentiFM economic event dataset collection and annotation. The annotated dataset consists of an English and Dutch news corpus. While in this paper the focus is on English, we refer to Lefever and Hoste (2016) for a pilot study on Dutch event detection and a description of the Dutch event data. A reference to where to download the SentiFM dataset can be found in Section 7.

The goal of the SentiFM dataset is to enable supervised data-driven event detection in company-specific economic news. For English, we downloaded articles from the newspaper The Financial Times using the ProQuest Newsstand by means of keyword-search. The keywords were manually determined based on a subsample of random articles as being indicative to one of the event types. All articles were published between November 2004 and November 2013. The articles had at least one of the following seven companies in the title: Barclays, BHP, Unilever, British Land, Tesco, Vodafone, and BASF. These companies were selected because they are highly ranked in several market indexes while situated in different sectors/industries. This facilitates corpus collection as there is more news content due to the companies' status. Sectorial diversification is necessary to avoid specialization to one particular industry. For instance, six out of 10 highest market cap companies in the S&P500 index currently belong to the IT sector. In total, we collected 497 news articles containing 2522 annotated company-specific economic events.

In the corpus, 10 types of company-specific economic events were manually identified:

Buy ratings A recommendation to purchase the security from an analyst. As event mentions, we include rating announcements, forecasts, performance, buy/sell/hold advice, and rating upgrades/downgrades/maintained.

Debt Event mentions pertaining to company debt and debt ratios. We include debt announcements, forecasts, increases, reductions, and restructuring.

Dividend A dividend is a distribution of a portion of a company's earnings paid to its shareholders. We include dividend announcements, forecasts, payments, none payments, stable yields, raises, and reductions.

Merger & acquisition Mergers and acquisitions refers to the consolidation of companies or assets involving at least two companies. We include announcements, forecasts, and cancellations of a merger/acquisition.

Profit Financial benefits that are realized when the amount of revenue exceeds expenses. We include declarations and forecasts of profit, positive and negative (losses) profit, lower than, higher than, as expected, increased, decreased, and stable profits.

Quarterly results Events pertaining to the quarterly report as a set of financial statements issued by a company. We include declaration of publication, forecasts, strong, weak, improved, declined, stable, better than, worse than, and as expected results.

Sales volume The quantity of goods and services sold over a certain period. We include declarations and predictions of sales volumes figures, increased, decreased, stable, better than, worse than, as expected sales volumes.

Share repurchase Share buyback events by a company including announcements and forecasts of share repurchases.

Target price Events on the projected price level of a security. We include announcements, forecasts, price raised, reduced, or maintained.

Turnover The number and frequency of securities traded over a certain period. We include declaration and prediction of turnover figures, increased, decreased, stable, worse than, better than, and as expected turnover.

These events and activities pertain to the specific instances of companies mentioned in the articles. The event typology was manually and iteratively constructed on a corpus subsample by an economic domain specialist. It is notable that this event typology overlaps largely with the independently created StockSonar typology (Feldman et al., 2011) and SPEED ontology (Hogenboom et al., 2013). These studies also used a manual and iterative approach to constructing a descriptive typology of company-specific economic events. It is unsurprising that the event types are highly similar.

Human annotators marked all mentions of each of these event types at the token level, using the Brat rapid annotation tool (Stenetorp et al., 2012), a web-based tool for text annotation. Events are linked to the earliest preceding company mentions with an 'about_company' relation (this relation is duplexed into 'acquiring_company' and 'target_company' for Merger & acquisition events). Discontinuous token spans and annotating multiple event types are allowed. Two annotators were involved in the first pass annotation phase. The gold standard was subsequently produced by an adjudication phase. The event annotation guidelines for English were ported from Dutch. To assess the reliability of the event annotations, we measured inter-annotator F_1-score on the events marked by 3 individual annotators in 10 articles from the Dutch corpus (consisting of 216 sentences and 3,202 tokens). With a cross-averaged F_1-score of 78.41% for the 3 annotator pairs, we can conclude that the annotated corpus is a reliable dataset for the task of economic event detection.

All texts were pre-processed (tokenized and sentence-splitted) using the LeTs Preprocess Toolkit (Van de Kauter et al., 2013).

The present task is sentence-level detection of event types, so one sentence instance can be assigned multiple event classes. Multiple labels are assigned to 3.81% ($n = 380$) of all sentence instances. An overview of the different event types and their total frequency is given in Table 1.

Figure 1: Annotated sentence examples from the Brat annotation tool.

Event type	Type ratio	# sentence instances
No Event	NA	7823 (75.62%)
BuyRating	9.00%	227 (2.19%)
Debt	2.38%	60 (0.58%)
Dividend	7.22%	182 (1.76%)
MergerAcquisition	10.03%	253 (2.45%)
Profit	25.81%	651 (6.29%)
QuarterlyResults	10.59%	267 (2.58%)
SalesVolume	19.31%	487 (4.71%)
ShareRepurchase	2.42%	61 (0.59%)
TargetPrice	3.73%	94 (0.91%)
Turnover	9.52%	240 (2.32%)
Total		2522 events/10345 sentences (24.38%)

Table 1: Event type distribution in the SentiFM English economic dataset and sentence level counts (as used in experiments).

3   Experimental Set-up

For this study, the task of economic event detection is conceived as a sentence-level classification task. We decided on comparing two different machine learning approaches: an SVM approach requiring offline feature engineering, and a word-vector-based sequence RNN-LSTM approach.

The SVM approach incorporates a rich feature set with syntactic and lexical feature engineering. We built one SVM classifier per event, predicting whether the event was present in the sentence or not, in effect recasting the problem as a one-vs-rest binary classification task for each class. The RNN-LSTM is tested both as a multi-label single model classifier and a one-vs-rest set-up.

Performance estimation is done on a random hold-out test split (10%), whereas cross-validation experiments were carried out on the hold-in set (train set of 90%) for both hyper-parameter optimization and validation of generalization error.

Per event type, precision, recall, and F_1-score are reported for each approach on the hold-out test set. We do not report accuracy because it is not an apt performance indicator in the case of class imbalance. Cross-validation results on the training set are not reported due to space constraints, but followed the same trends as the reported test results with no indication of over-fitting.

3.1   Support Vector Machines

For the first set of experiments, a support vector machine model was built per economic event type in a one-vs-rest set-up applying two different kernels: (1) the *linear* kernel with default LIBSVM hyperparameters and (2) a hyper-parameter optimized version of the *RBF* kernel. The optimal weights for the c and g parameters for the RBF kernel were obtained by means of a 5-fold grid search on the training data for each event type. All experiments were carried out with the LIBSVM package (Chang and Lin, 2011).

In a first step, the data set was linguistically pre-processed by means of the LeTs Preprocessing Toolkit (Van de Kauter et al., 2013), which performs lemmatization, part-of-speech tagging, and named entity recognition. Consequently, a set of lexical and syntactic features were constructed on the basis of the pre-processed data.

Lexical features   The following lexical features were constructed: token n-gram features (unigrams, bigrams and trigrams), character n-gram features (trigrams and fourgrams), lemma n-gram features (unigrams, bigrams and trigrams), disambiguated lemmas (lemma + associated PoS-tag), and a set of features indicating the presence of numerals, symbols, and time indicators (e.g. *yesterday*).

Syntactic features   As syntactic features, we extracted three features for each PoS-category: binary (presence of category in the instance), ternary (category occurs 0, 1 or more times in the instance) and total number of occurrences of the respective PoS-label. In addition, similar features (binary, ternary, and frequency) were extracted for 6 different Named Entity types: person, organization, location, product, event, and miscellaneous.

3.2 Recurrent Neural Net LSTM

The RNN-LSTM approach was implemented using the Keras neural networks API (Chollet et al., 2015) with TensorFlow as back-end (Abadi et al., 2015). We employ a straightforward neural architecture: the input-layer is a trainable embedding layer which feeds into an LSTM block. The LSTM block is connected to an output layer with a sigmoid activation function. Bi-directionality of the LSTM-layer is tested in hyper-parameter optimization. We use the Adam optimization algorithm with binary cross-entropy loss function. The embedding layer turns positive integers, in our case hold-in set token indexes, in dense vectors with fixed dimensionality. An existing word embedding matrix can be used in the input-layer which tunes pre-trained word vectors.

Three embedded inputs were tested with the multi-label set-up: 200 dimensional GloVe (Pennington et al., 2014) word vectors trained on the hold-in set, 300 dimensional GloVe vectors trained on a 6 billion token corpus of Wikipedia (2014) + Gigawords5B[1] (henceforth, 6B corpus), and no pre-trained embeddings. The latter means our classifier trains embedded word-representations (with a fixed dimensionality of 200) itself based on the token sequences of the hold-in set. We evaluated our own GloVe models on an analogy quality assessment task provided with the word2vec source code[2]. We picked the highest dimensional word vector model from the top ten ranking on the analogy task. We excluded lower dimensional vectors because preliminary tests have shown that higher dimensional pre-trained vectors obtained better scores.

We first tested a multi-label and subsequently a one-vs-rest approach in which a binary classifier is trained for each economic event class. The multi-label approach requires one full training iteration compared to one for each of the 10 classes in one-vs-rest and is much less computationally expensive. For this reason we limit the tested word-

[1] https://nlp.stanforth.edu/projects/glove/
[2] https://code.google.com/archive/p/word2vec/

vector inputs to the 6B GloVe word vectors in the one-vs-rest approach. These input vectors outperformed others in the multi-label experiments considering F_1-score per label, as well as the hold-in set vectors in preliminary tests using limited iteration randomized search testing.

The following model hyper-parameters were set by 3-fold random search with 32 iterations. The winning hyper-parameters are chosen by prevalence-weighted macro-averaged F_1-score over the multi-label prediction.

RNN-LSTM hyper-parameter	Setting
Bidirectionality on LSTM layer	Enabled or disabled
LSTM unit size	$d \in \{134, 268, 536\}$
Dropout rate	$r \in \{0.0, 0.2\}$
Recurrent dropout rate	$rr \in \{0.0, 0.2\}$
Batch size	$b \in \{64, 128, 256, 512\}$
Training epochs	$e \in \{32, 64, 128\}$

Table 2: RNN-LSTM model hyper-parameters.

In the next section, the best model hyper-parametrization as determined by prevalence-weighted macro-averaged F_1-score will be discussed.

4 Experimental Results

We present per class results of the SVM one-vs-rest approach in Table 3 and for the RNN-LSTM in Table 4 for multi-label and Table 5 for one-vs-rest. Even though our classifiers were trained on a limited amount of data, we obtain satisfactory results for the detection of company-specific economic events for most event types. Overall precision scores are promising, especially for the SVM-based approach and the RNN-LSTM with hold-in trained word vectors.

The best overall results are obtained by the linear kernel SVM which obtained far better recall than any other model. The one-vs-rest RNN-LSTM systems comes in at a close second and outperforms its multi-label counterparts by a large margin. Including lexical and syntactic features seems to be worthwhile when compared to the straight-forward word vector/token sequence approach used with the RNN-LSTM.

The best RNN-LSTM multi-label model is outperformed by the linear kernel SVM approach and is on par with the optimized RBF kernel approach. The pre-trained GloVe vectors trained on our own dataset performed best out of the three input methods with a prevalence-weighted macro-averaged F_1-score of 0.66 on hold-out. The GloVe vectors trained on the 6B corpus obtain worse precision but slightly better recall, resulting in a comparable F_1-score of 0.64. The 6B GloVe inputs obtain better scores on more classes, but their macro-averaged score is hurt by not detecting any of the Debt class instances. Not feeding pre-trained embeddings to our network shows the worst performance of all classifiers (F_1-score of 0.54).

Event type	Precision	Recall	F_1-score
Linear kernel one-vs-rest			
BuyRating	<u>**0.95**</u>	**0.91**	<u>**0.93**</u>
Debt	**0.50**	<u>**1.00**</u>	<u>**0.67**</u>
Dividend	**0.62**	<u>**0.73**</u>	<u>**0.67**</u>
MergerAcquisition	**0.56**	**0.40**	**0.47**
Profit	0.75	0.74	0.75
QuarterlyResults	0.82	0.53	0.64
SalesVolume	0.88	**0.75**	<u>**0.81**</u>
ShareRepurchase	<u>**1.00**</u>	0.50	0.67
TargetPrice	<u>**1.00**</u>	0.75	0.86
Turnover	**0.91**	<u>**0.77**</u>	<u>**0.83**</u>
avg	<u>**0.80**</u>	<u>**0.71**</u>	**0.73**

Event type	Precision	Recall	F_1-score
Optimized RBF one-vs-rest			
BuyRating	<u>**0.95**</u>	**0.91**	<u>**0.93**</u>
Debt	**0.50**	<u>**1.00**</u>	<u>**0.67**</u>
Dividend	0.54	0.64	0.58
MergerAcquisition	0.00	0.00	0.00
Profit	**0.80**	**0.76**	**0.78**
QuarterlyResults	**0.83**	**0.56**	**0.67**
SalesVolume	<u>**0.94**</u>	0.65	0.77
ShareRepurchase	<u>**1.00**</u>	**0.50**	**0.67**
TargetPrice	<u>**1.00**</u>	**0.75**	**0.86**
Turnover	0.87	**0.77**	0.82
avg	0.74	0.65	0.67

Table 3: Hold-out test precision, recall, and F_1-scores per type for the linear and optimized RBF kernels of the feature-engineered SVM one-vs-rest approach. **Boldface** indicates best performance within the SVM set-up. <u>Underline</u> indicates best of all tested systems.

Event type	Precision	Recall	F_1-score
Hold-in set GloVe multi-label			
BuyRating	**0.91**	**0.91**	**0.91**
Debt	<u>**1.00**</u>	**0.50**	<u>**0.67**</u>
Dividend	0.50	0.36	0.42
MergerAcquisition	0.32	0.24	0.27
Profit	0.75	<u>**0.81**</u>	0.78
QuarterlyResults	<u>**0.87**</u>	0.38	0.53
SalesVolume	**0.92**	0.67	0.77
ShareRepurchase	0.80	**0.67**	0.73
TargetPrice	<u>**1.00**</u>	**0.50**	**0.67**
Turnover	<u>**0.95**</u>	0.69	0.80
avg	<u>**0.80**</u>	0.57	**0.66**

Event type	Precision	Recall	F_1-score
6B corpus GloVe multi-label			
BuyRating	0.86	0.82	0.84
Debt	0.00	0.00	0.00
Dividend	0.50	**0.55**	0.52
MergerAcquisition	**0.40**	**0.32**	**0.36**
Profit	0.82	0.79	<u>**0.81**</u>
QuarterlyResults	0.77	<u>**0.68**</u>	<u>**0.72**</u>
SalesVolume	0.84	**0.73**	0.78
ShareRepurchase	<u>**1.00**</u>	<u>**0.67**</u>	<u>**0.80**</u>
TargetPrice	0.75	0.75	**0.75**
Turnover	0.90	**0.73**	**0.81**
avg	0.68	**0.60**	0.64

Event type	Precision	Recall	F_1-score
No pre-trained word vectors multi-label			
BuyRating	0.81	0.59	0.68
Debt	0.33	0.50	0.40
Dividend	<u>**0.75**</u>	**0.55**	**0.63**
MergerAcquisition	0.21	0.12	0.15
Profit	<u>**0.83**</u>	0.33	0.47
QuarterlyResults	0.67	0.35	0.46
SalesVolume	0.86	0.61	0.71
ShareRepurchase	0.60	0.50	0.55
TargetPrice	**1.00**	**0.50**	**0.67**
Turnover	0.88	0.58	0.70
avg	0.69	0.46	0.54

Table 4: Hold-out test precision, recall, and F_1-scores per type for RNN-LSTM for different word vector input. **Boldface** indicates best performance within RNN-LSTM multi-label approach. <u>Underline</u> indicates best of all systems.

In both one-vs-rest approaches, we trade off computation time for performance compared to multi-label systems. This approach also has the advantage that a separate classifier is produced for each class. At prediction time, we can thus trivially apply the best available classifier algorithm from both the SVM and RNN-LSTM systems for each class. When combining classifiers in this manner an average score of 0.81% precision, 0.74% recall, and 0.75% F_1-score is reached, improving over the best scoring single algorithm system.

5 Error Analysis

We performed a detailed error analysis on the best classifier in order to gain insights in the main shortcomings of the current approach.

Event type	Precision	Recall	F_1-score
6B corpus GloVe one-vs-rest			
BuyRating	0.88	<u>0.95</u>	0.91
Debt	0.50	0.50	0.50
Dividend	0.55	0.55	0.55
MergerAcquisition	<u>0.58</u>	<u>0.44</u>	<u>0.50</u>
Profit	0.81	0.74	0.77
QuarterlyResults	0.84	0.47	0.60
SalesVolume	0.81	<u>0.76</u>	0.79
ShareRepurchase	0.75	0.50	0.60
TargetPrice	<u>1.00</u>	<u>1.00</u>	<u>1.00</u>
Turnover	0.94	0.65	0.77
avg	0.77	0.66	0.70

Table 5: Hold-out test precision, recall, and F_1-scores per type for the one-vs-rest RNN-LSTM with 6B GloVe corpus word vectors. <u>Underline</u> indicates best of all systems.

In general, we noticed that a fair amount of event types are characterized by strong lexical clues. As an example, we can cite the following *BuyRating* example, where the unigrams *upgraded*, *hold* and *buy* can be considered lexical indicators of this category:

(1) *Repair and maintenance group Homeserve, which also reports on Friday, rose 2.8 per cent to pound(s)17.54 after RBS upgraded from "hold" to "buy".*

Most of the event categories, however, show a **large variety of possible lexicalizations**. This is illustrated by examples 2 and 3 for SalesVolume, examples 4 and 5 for ShareRepurchase, and examples 6, 7 and 8 for Turnover:

(2) *This could raise doubts about Vodafone's target of reaching 10m subscribers by the end of the current financial year.*

(3) *It will increase the number of Barclays' customers in France by 25 per cent.*

(4) *Last week, Engelhard scotched hopes of a negotiated deal with BASF, after three months of ding-dong talks, unveiling instead a defence strategy centred on a planned Dollars 1.2bn share buy-back at Dollars 45 a share.*

(5) *So far, free cash flow has been used to finance share buybacks and dividend increases.*

(6) *The mobile network reseller also forecast mid-teen percentage growth in service revenue, far better than most analysts had expected in a tough UK market.*

(7) *However, revenues from voice and text fell in the period.*

(8) *Arun Sarin yesterday sought to dispel fears about slowing revenue growth at Vodafone by saying the mobile phone company would make more acquisitions in Africa and Asia.*

In addition, some of the lexical clues are **ambiguous** in the sense that they occur with various event categories. This is for instance the case for *buy*, which can be informative to predict the *BuyRating* (Example 9) as well as the *MergerAcquisition* (Example 10) event categories:

(9) *EMI eased 1.19 per cent to 252p in spite of a buy recommendation from Deutsche Bank.*

(10) *G4S led the blue-chip risers amid continued speculation that shareholders may block its pound(s)5.2bn deal to buy ISS, the office cleaning group.*

In future work, we intend to improve the lexical coverage by increasing the data set size, but also by adding semantic knowledge from structured resources. The following *BuyRating* event has not been detected, but this could be the case if *downgrade* could be correctly identified as a lowering in rating (viz. moving the rating from a buy to a hold, or a hold to a sell).

(11) *The weak oil price and a downgrade from RBS did the damage.*

The same holds for the following *MergerAcquisition* example, where *takeover* should be semantically clustered together with *acquire, acquisition,* etc.

(12) *News that Hewlett-Packard was preparing a $10bn takeover offer for the software maker came too late for London traders to react.*

Furthermore, for some event categories, the evaluation set is too limited to draw reliable conclusions. As can be noticed in Table 6, which lists the number of instances per category in the test set, the *Debt* and *TargetPrice* evaluation sets contain less than five test items. Collecting and annotating

Event type	# test instances
BuyRating	22
Debt	2
Dividend	11
MergerAcquisition	25
Profit	58
QuarterlyResults	34
SalesVolume	51
ShareRepurchase	6
TargetPrice	4
Turnover	26
Total	994

Table 6: Economic event type distribution in the evaluation set.

additional data should lead to a better coverage for all event categories.

Another source of wrong classification was due to annotation errors in the data set. This is illustrated by Example 13, where the *buyRating* event was not labeled, and Example 14, where the *dividend* label was lacking:

(13) *Morgan Stanley repeated " underweight " advice in a note sent to clients overnight .*

(14) *ECS argues Verizon Wireless is a "passive investment" for Vodafone because it last received a dividend in 2004-05, worth Pounds 923m.*

Finally, the error analysis also revealed that some strong lexical clues are not always picked up by the classifier to correctly predict the event category. We assume this might be due to the very large feature space, as the SVM classifier is now trained on more than 300,000 bag-of-words features. In addition to the skewed data distribution, this large feature set makes the machine learning task very challenging. Therefore, we expect the classification performance to improve by performing feature selection to determine which sources of information are most relevant for solving this learning task. Having a good mechanism to select informative bag-of-words features should allow to correctly predict the economic event in case lexical clues are present in the sentence. In this case, the following sentence should definitely be classified as a *MergerAcquisition* event:

(15) *The acquisition would give CIBC control of FirstCaribbean with a stake of 87.4 per cent .*

6   Conclusions

This paper presents a dataset and classification experiments for company-specific economic event detection in English news articles. Currently, there is little to no data resources and experiments for supervised, data-driven economic event extraction. The task was approached as a supervised classification approach and two different machine learning algorithms, an SVM and RNN-LSTM learner, were tested for the task. For our SentiFM event dataset, we have shown that a feature-engineered SVM approach obtains better performance than an RNN-LSTM word-vector system. The results show good classification performance for most event types, with the linear kernel SVM outperforming the RBF kernel SVM and RNN-LSTM set-ups. We demonstrated that data-driven approaches obtain good recall and can capture variation in lexicalizations of events to a satisfactory extent.

There is still plenty of room for improvement: more annotated data and augmentative resources are needed to further offset ambiguous event expressions. In future work, we will design a more fine-grained event detection model that also extracts the token span of the event below the sentence level. Furthermore, we will work on detecting subevents currently contained in our annotations: e.g. BuyRating: outperform, hold, sell, upgrade, etc. As feature engineering seems to pay off for the extraction of economic events, we will integrate additional linguistic information by adding semantic knowledge from structured resources such as DBpedia and dedicated ontologies for economics (e.g. the NewsEvent ontology (Lösch and Nikitina, 2009) and derived CoProE ontology (Kakkonen and Mufti, 2011)) as well as syntactic information extracted from dependency parses.

7   Data availability

The SentiFM company-specific economic news event dataset and annotation guidelines as used in this paper are available for download from `https://osf.io/enu2k/` (Van de Kauter et al., 2018). This repository also contains replication data including the vectorized feature data and test split.

8 Acknowledgment

The work presented in this paper was carried out in the framework of the SENTiVENT project aspirant grant of the Research Foundation - Flanders.

References

Martín Abadi, Ashish Agarwal, Paul Barham, Eugene Brevdo, Zhifeng Chen, Craig Citro, Greg S. Corrado, Andy Davis, Jeffrey Dean, Matthieu Devin, Sanjay Ghemawat, Ian Goodfellow, Andrew Harp, Geoffrey Irving, Michael Isard, Yangqing Jia, Rafal Jozefowicz, Lukasz Kaiser, Manjunath Kudlur, Josh Levenberg, Dan Mané, Rajat Monga, Sherry Moore, Derek Murray, Chris Olah, Mike Schuster, Jonathon Shlens, Benoit Steiner, Ilya Sutskever, Kunal Talwar, Paul Tucker, Vincent Vanhoucke, Vijay Vasudevan, Fernanda Viégas, Oriol Vinyals, Pete Warden, Martin Wattenberg, Martin Wicke, Yuan Yu, and Xiaoqiang Zheng. 2015. TensorFlow: Large-scale machine learning on heterogeneous systems.

Jacqueline Aguilar, Charley Beller, Paul McNamee, Benjamin Van Durme, Stephanie Strassel, Zhiyi Song, and Joe Ellis. 2014. A comparison of the events and relations across ACE, ERE, TAC-KBP, and FrameNet annotation standards. In *Proceedings of the Second Workshop on EVENTS: Definition, Detection, Coreference, and Representation*, pages 45–53.

David Ahn. 2006. The stages of event extraction. In *Proceedings of the Workshop on Annotating and Reasoning about Time and Events*, pages 1–8. Association for Computational Linguistics.

Ernest Arendarenko and Tuomo Kakkonen. 2012. Ontology-Based Information and Event Extraction for Business Intelligence. In *Artificial Intelligence: Methodology, Systems, and Applications*, volume 7557 of *Lecture Notes in Computer Science*, pages 89–102. Springer.

Zvi Ben Ami and Ronen Feldman. 2017. Event-based trading: Building superior trading strategies with state-of-the-art information extraction tools. SSRN Working Paper 2907600.

Jacob Boudoukh, Ronen Feldman, Shimon Kogan, and Matthew P Richardson. 2016. Information, trading, and volatility: Evidence from firm-specific news. SSRN Working Paper 2193667.

Chih-Chung Chang and Chih-Jen Lin. 2011. LIBSVM: A Library for Support Vector Machines. *ACM Transactions on Intelligent Systems and Technology (TIST)*, 2:27:1–27:27.

François Chollet et al. 2015. Keras. https://github.com/fchollet/keras.

Xiao Ding, Yue Zhang, Ting Liu, and Junwen Duan. 2015. Deep learning for event-driven stock prediction. In *Proceedings of the 24th International Conference on Artificial Intelligence*, IJCAI'15, pages 2327–2333. AAAI Press.

Mian Du, Lidia Pivovarova, and Roman Yangarber. 2016. PULS: natural language processing for business intelligence. In *Proceedings of the 2016 Workshop on Human Language Technology*, pages 1–8.

Robert F. Engle and Victor K. Ng. 1993. Measuring and Testing the Impact of News on Volatility. *The Journal of Finance*, 48(5):1749–1778.

Ronen Feldman, Benjamin Rosenfeld, Roy Bar-Haim, and Moshe Fresko. 2011. The stock sonarsentiment analysis of stocks based on a hybrid approach. In *Twenty-Third IAAI Conference*.

Alexander Hogenboom, Frederik Hogenboom, Flavius Frasincar, Kim Schouten, and Otto van der Meer. 2013. Semantics-Based Information Extraction for Detecting Economic Events. *Multimedia Tools and Applications*, 64(1):27–52.

Tuomo Kakkonen and Tabish Mufti. 2011. Developing and applying a company, product and business event ontology for text mining. In *Proceedings of the 11th International Conference on Knowledge Management and Knowledge Technologies*, page 24. ACM.

Marjan Van de Kauter, Geert Coorman, Els Lefever, Bart Desmet, Lieve Macken, and Véronique Hoste. 2013. LeTs Preprocess: The multilingual LT3 linguistic preprocessing toolkit. *Computational Linguistics in the Netherlands Journal*, 3:103–120.

Marjan Van de Kauter, Gilles Jacobs, Els Lefever, and Vronique Hoste. 2018. SentiFM company-specific economic news event dataset (English).

Els Lefever and Veronique Hoste. 2016. A classification-based approach to economic event detection in dutch news text. In *Proceedings of the Tenth International Conference on Language Resources and Evaluation (LREC '16)*, pages 330–335. European Language Resources Association (ELRA).

Uta Lösch and Nadejda Nikitina. 2009. The newsEvents ontology: an ontology for describing business events. In *Proceedings of the 2009 International Conference on Ontology Patterns-Volume 516*, pages 187–193. CEUR-WS. org.

A. Craig MacKinlay. 1997. Event Studies in Economics and Finance. *Journal of Economic Literature*, 35(1):13–39.

Ghulam Mujtaba Mian and Srinivasan Sankaraguruswamy. 2012. Investor Sentiment and Stock Market Response to Earnings News. *The Accounting Review*, 87(4):1357–1384.

Teruko Mitamura, Zhengzhong Liu, and Eduard Hovy. 2016. Overview of TAC-KBP 2016 event nugget track. In *Text Analysis Conference*.

Jeffrey Pennington, Richard Socher, and Christopher D. Manning. 2014. Glove: Global vectors for word representation. In *Empirical Methods in Natural Language Processing (EMNLP)*, pages 1532–1543.

Samuel Rönnqvist and Peter Sarlin. 2017. Bank distress in the news: Describing events through deep learning. *Neurocomputing*, 264:57–70.

Rachele Sprugnoli and Sara Tonelli. 2017. One, no one and one hundred thousand events: Defining and processing events in an inter-disciplinary perspective. *Natural Language Engineering*, 23(4):485–506.

Pontus Stenetorp, Sampo Pyysalo, Goran Topić, Tomoko Ohta, Sophia Ananiadou, and Jun'ichi Tsujii. 2012. brat: a Web-based Tool for NLP-Assisted Text Annotation. In *Proceedings of the 13th Conference of the European Chapter of the Association for Computational Linguistics (EACL'12)*, pages 102–107, Avignon, France.

Paul C. Tetlock. 2007. Giving Content to Investor Sentiment: The Role of Media in the Stock Market. *The Journal of Finance*, 62(3):1139–1168.

Boyi Xie, Rebecca J. Passonneau, Leon Wu, and Germán G. Creamer. 2013. Semantic frames to predict stock price movement. In *Proceedings of the 51st Annual Meeting of the Association for Computational Linguistics (Volume 1: Long Papers)*, pages 873–883. Association for Computational Linguistics.

Causality Analysis of Twitter Sentiments and Stock Market Returns

Narges Tabari
nseyedit@uncc.edu
UNC Charlotte

Bhanu Praneeth
bsirukur@uncc.edu
UNC Charlotte

Piyusha Biswas
pbiswas1@uncc.edu
UNC Charlotte

Armin Seyeditabari
sseyedi1@uncc.edu
UNC Charlotte

Mirsad Hadzikadic
Mirsad@uncc.edu
UNC Charlotte

Wlodek Zadrozny
wzadrozn@uncc.edu
UNC Charlotte

Abstract

Sentiment analysis is the process of identifying the opinion expressed in text. Recently, it has been used to study behavioral finance, and in particular the effect of opinions and emotions on economic or financial decisions. In this paper, we use a public dataset of labeled tweets that has been labeled by Amazon Mechanical Turk and then we propose a baseline classification model. Then, by using Granger causality of both sentiment datasets with the different stocks, we shows that there is causality between social media and stock market returns (in both directions) for many stocks. Finally, We evaluate this causality analysis by showing that in the event of a specific news on certain dates, there are evidences of trending the same news on Twitter for that stock.

1 Introduction

Sentiment analysis of Twitter messages has been used to study behavioral finance, specifically, the effect of sentiments driven from social media on financial and economical decisions. For example, Bollen and Pepe 2011 used social-media sentiment analysis to predict the size of markets, while Antenucci et al. 2014 used it to predict unemployment rates over time. Twitter sentiment analysis in particular, is a challenging task because its text contains many misspelled words, abbreviation, grammatical errors, and made up words. Therefore, it contains limited contextual information.

In previous research, it was implied that if it is properly modeled, Twitter can be used to forecast useful information about the market. Tharsis et al.

used a Twitter sentiment analysis from (Kolchyna et al., 2015) which was SVM approach, then compared them to different industries and showed that by adding the sentiments to their predictive models, the error rate reduced between 1 to 3 percent, in predicting the Expected Returns of different industries (Souza et al., 2015). Alanyali et al. found a positive correlation between the number of mentions of a company in the Financial Times and the volume of its stock (Alanyali et al., 2013). There has been many related research in this area, but there are shortcomings that needs to be specified. First, datasets used for sentiment analysis, is not specifically in context of finance (Bollen and Pepe, 2011; Souza et al., 2015). Secondly, the classification models mostly have low accuracy (Bollen and Pepe, 2011; Loughran and Mcdonald, 2010; Ranco et al., 2015; Lillo et al., 2012).

In our research on investigation on impacts of social media and stock market, we pulled a dataset of tweet in duration of three months that was labeled by both Amazon mechanical Turk, and then again we designed a classification model using SVM, with 79.9% of accuracy. Then, Granger Causality analysis of these two tweet datasets with various stock returns has shown that for many companies theres a statistical significant causality between stock and the sentiments driven from tweets in different lags. When evaluating this relation, we realized that on specific dates that jumps in stock market return occur, there are many evidence of mentions of the same news in our Twitter dataset which caused the change in stock market return

In Section 2, we will describe the dataset that was pulled from Twitter, pre-processing techniques, labels by Amazon Mechanical Turk, and the machine learning classifier. This section has been also used in another analysis which is cur-

Proceedings of the First Workshop on Economics and Natural Language Processing, pages 11–19
Melbourne, Australia, July 20, 2018. ©2018 Association for Computational Linguistics

rently under review to ECML-PKDD 2018. In section three, we explain the causality models, and results. And finally, in section five, we describe the evaluation process. We conclude our findings in section six.

2 Data

Tweets were pulled from Twitter using Twitter API between 1/1/2017 and 3/31/2017. In our filters, we only pulled tweets that are tweeted from a "Verified" account. A verified account on Twitter suggests that the account is a public interest and that it is authentic. An account gets verified by Twitter if the used is a distinguished person in different key interest areas, such as politics, journalism, government, music, business, and others. A Tweet were considered stock related if it contains at least one of the stock symbols of the first 100 most frequent stock symbols that were included in SemEval dataset form (Cortis et al., 2017). We were able to pull 20,013 tweets in that interval using mentioned filters.

2.1 Labeling using Amazon Mechanical Turk

The data was submitted to Amazon Mechanical Turk, was asked to be labeled by 4 different workers. Snow et al. 2008 suggested that 4 workers is enough to make sure that enough people have submitted their opinion on each tweet and so the results would be reliable. We assigned only AMT masters as our workers, meaning they have the highest performance in performing wide range of HITs (Human Intelligence Tasks). We also asked the workers to assign sentiments based on the question: "Is the tweet beneficial to the stock mentioned in tweet or not?". It was important that tweet is not labeled based on perspective of how beneficial it would be for the investor; rather how beneficial it would be to the company itself. Each worker assigned numbers from -2 (very negative) to +2 (very positive) to each tweet. Table 1 shows the inter-rater percentage agreement between sentiments assigned to each tweets by the four different workers. We considered labels 'very positive' and 'positive' as positive when calculating the inter-agreement percentage.

At the end, the average of the four sentiment was assigned to each tweet as the final sentiment. Out of 20013 tweet records submitted to AMT, we assigned neutral sentiment to a tweet if it had average score between [-0.5, +0.5]. We picked the sen-

Table 1: Percentage agreement between four workers.

Workers	Agreement
(1, 2)	82.3%
(1, 3)	84.5%
(1, 4)	82.2%
(2, 3)	84.3%
(2, 4)	81.9%
(3, 4)	82.1%

Table 2: Summary of tweets labeled by Amazon Mechanical Turk.

Range	Label assigned to tweets	Count
[-2, -0.5]	Negative	2082
[-0.5, 0.5]	Neutral	9008
[0.5, 2]	Positive	8386

timent positive/negative if at least half of workers labeled them positive/negative. Table 2 is a summary of the number of tweets in each category of sentiment.

2.2 Classification Model

We used Amazon Mechanical Turk to manually label our stock market tweets. In order to create a classification model, so it can be used to predict more tweets in the future analysis, we applied the same preprocessing technique and classification models explained in detail by Tabari et. al Tabari et al. (2017). In preprocessing phase, after tokenization, all numbers were substituted with <num> tag. Also, some characters were removed from the text, such as '-' and '.'. Then, to create our feature set, We modified Loughran's lexicon of positive and negative words (Loughran and Mcdonald, 2010) to be suited for stock market context and used it to calculate number of positive or negative words in each tweet as feature. For example, 'sell' has a negative sentiment in stock market context, that has been added to Loughran's lexicon. We ultimately added around 120 new words to their list which is added in Appendix A. Also, as another feature, we replaced couple of words that come together in a tweet, but has different sentiment in stock market context, with one specific word. For example, 'Go down' and 'Pull back' both contain negative sentiment in stock's perceptive. Around 90 word-couples was defined specifically for this content and are mentioned in Appendix B. Table 3, shows the result for different machine learning classifiers.

3 Causality Models

3.1 Granger Causality

Granger Causality (GC) is a probabilistic approach for determining if information about past of one variable can explain another and it is based on aversion of the probabilistic theory of causality (Hitchcock, 2016). According to Suppes (Suppes, 1970), an event A causes prima facie an event B if the conditional probability of B given A is greater than the probability of B alone, and A occurs before B. which is a very common approach in econometrics. Clive Granger has expanded on this in what is now known as Granger Causality (Granger and Aug, 1969).

Granger Causality: a variable A causes B if the probability of B conditional on its own past history and the past history of A does not equal the probability of B conditional on its past history alone. Advantage of this model is that it is operational and easy to implement. Although, the definition is not really one of causality but of increased predictability which is not really the same thing. There are plenty of people who criticize this definition and point out that A can Granger Cause B but controlling A might not imply that we can directly influence B or that we even know the magnitude of what will happen to B. Granger Causality is mainly important for causal notions for policy control, explanation and understanding of time-series, and in some cases for prediction.

Correlation is not causation It is important to understand that correlation is different than causation. Correlation means that there is relationship between two sets of variables, where change in one, causes change in the other variable. Whereas we describe causation in way that previous information about one time-series can help explaining the other variable. Two time-series can have causality but not any correlation between them and vice versa. Correlation is a symmetric relation a measure of statistical linear dependence but causality is an asymmetric relation.

Definition of Granger Causality: A time-series Y can be written as an autoregressive process in which the past values of Y are able to explain (in part) the current value of Y:

$$y_t = \alpha + \sum_{i=1}^{k} \beta_j Y_{t-i} + \epsilon_t. \tag{1}$$

Granger defined causality in the following way: Consider an other variable X which has past values as well. If the past values of X help improve the prediction of current values of Y beyond what we get with past values of Y alone, then X is said to Granger Cause Y . The test is under taken as:

$$y_t = \alpha + \sum_{i=1}^{k} \beta_j Y_{t-i} + \sum_{j}^{k} \lambda_j X_{t-j} + \epsilon_t. \tag{2}$$

The test is an F-test on all being jointly equal to zero for all values of J. If you reject the null hypothesis then X is said to Granger Cause Y. Note that it is entirely possible, and appropriate, to test whether Y can be said to Granger Cause X. It is possible for X to GC Y, Y to GC X, or for neither to influence the other. Granger causality tests should only be undertaken on I(0) variables, that is variables with a time-invariant mean and variance and that can be adequately represented by a linear AR(p) process, i.e. the time series must be stationary.

3.2 Stock market returns

For each 100 stock ticker symbol mentioned in the tweet dataset, the stock closing price were downloaded.[1] After that, for each company we calculated the relative daily return. Using return instead of closing price, creates a stationary time-series which is essential for most time-series analysis and specifically for Granger Causality. Relative return is the return an asset achieves over a period of time compared to a benchmark. [2] A relative return is a means to measure the performance of an active portfolio, compared to other investments.

---

[1] Out of 100 companies, we eliminated the stock symbols that were bought by other companies and instead used the current companys stock symbol. We eliminated $LNKD (LinkdIn) due to the fact that it was bought by $MSFT (Microsoft) and used Microsoft for both companies. Similarly, $SCTY (Solar City) was eliminated and $TSLA has taken into account for both companies. We also excluded the following companies from the list of 100 companies (VXX, GLD, SPY, GDX , SPX , WFM , EMC, APP, BRCM, and GMCR). These were either not currently trading or we could not find their trading data, or they were a specific index.

[2] https://www.investopedia.com

Table 3: Classification results.

Classifier	Feature Set	Accuracy
Random Forest	[TF-IDF]	78.6%
Random Forest	[TF-IDF, pos/neg count]	78.9%
Random Forest	[TF-IDF, pos/neg count, Word-couple]	79.4%
SVM	[TF-IDF]	77.9%
SVM	[TF-IDF, pos/neg count]	**79.9%**
SVM	[TF-IDF, pos/neg count, Word-couple]	79.5%

Relative stock return was calculate based on the following formula:

$$Stock return = \frac{(p_1 - p_0)}{p_0}$$
$$p_0 = Initial stock price \quad (3)$$
$$p_1 = Ending stock price$$

3.3 Comparison of social media sentiment analysis and stock market returns: Results

In order to use GC, we will first need to start with KPSS [3] test which is hypothesis testing for a time-series to be stationary. A stationary time series is where statistical properties such as mean and variance are constant over time. The null-hypothesis for the test is that the data is stationary; with an alternative that the data is not stationary. We applied this test for all three datasets, the two daily sentiment and the stock return. And then for each non-stationary dataset, we calculated the difference that would create a stationary time-series using the appropriate lag number. After KPSS testing, in the case that the p-value was greater than 0.05, the null hypothesis for data being stationary were not rejected. After making sure all three datasets are stationary, the following GC models were applied on both the sentiments predicted by our classifier in part 2.2 and labeled by AMT.

Model (1):
$$RV \sim Lags(RV, LAG) + Lags(SSC, LAG)$$
$$(4)$$

Model (2):
$$SSC \sim Lags(SSC, LAG) + Lags(RV, LAG)$$
$$(5)$$

Model one, is investigating if the stock returns cause sentiment scores and model 2 in the causal

---

[3]Kwiatkowski-Phillips-Schmidt-Shin: https://en.wikipedia.org/wiki/KPSS_test

impact of sentiment score on stock return. RV (Return Value) is the calculated daily return for 83 different stocks. We considered SSC (Sentiment Score) once for the sentiments predicted in part 2.2 and again for the one labeled by AMT. We used LAGs between 1 to 10 in our model. The goal was twofold, first to find out if the causal relationship is happening two way? Secondly, we wanted to determine the lag number that would explain causality for each model. The P-value, and F-value of all granger causality modes that at least was statistically significant in one direction is mentioned in Appendix C.

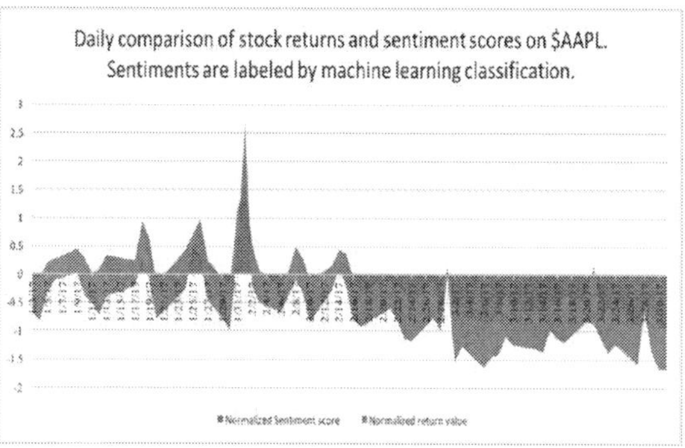

Figure 1: Daily comparison of stock returns and sentiment scores on $APPL. Sentiments are labeled by AMT. This shows that there is a general trend between stock return and the sentiments labeled by AMT.

Figure 1 is comparing the daily sentiments calculated by AMT and stock return and Figure 2 shows the same information with sentiments predicted using machine learning classification. These two figure are a good visualization proof that there is a trend between how stock market moves and sentiment score changes. Comparing these two shows two important points: first, the overall trend of the stock returns and sentiment for both, follow each other. Secondly, comparing two

14

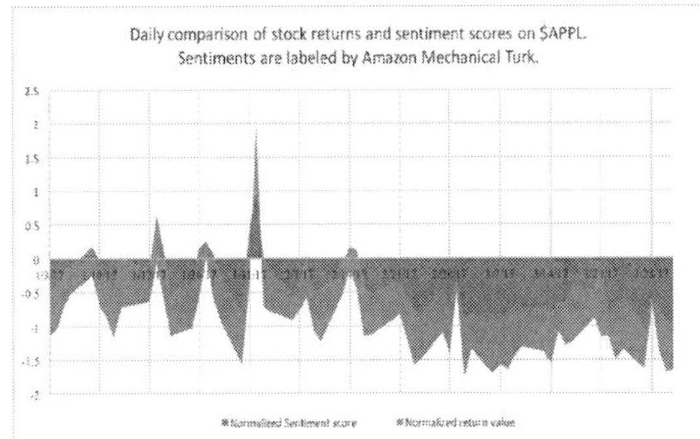

Figure 2: Daily comparison of stock returns and sentiment scores on $APPL. Sentiments are predicted by ML model. This shows that there is a general trend between stock return and the sentiments labeled by our machine learning model. Although the trend is not as obvious as the one with AMT, but it still exists. This is a visual representation of that 20% error rate is damaging the trend to some extend.

sentiment scores show that AMT has done a better job with the sentiments to our machine learning model. Therefore, decreasing the 20% error rate and improving the accuracy of the machine learning model is actually important and necessary.

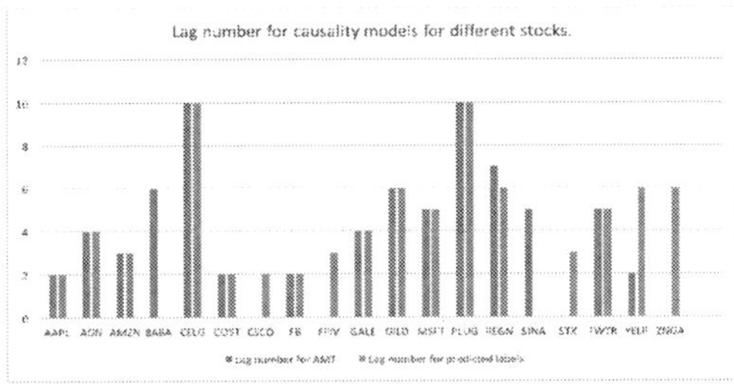

Figure 3: Lag number for GC for various stocks in model two. Lag is the number of days before current day that sentiment score had causal effect on stock market return.

Figure 3 is the plot of the lag number in which the Granger Causality model was statistically significant for different stocks in model two (Impact of sentiment results on stock market). Lag number is the number of the days before the current day, that had sentiment scores had causal effect on stock market return. The stocks with just one bar indicate that the causality model for the other sentiment dataset was not significant in any lags, meaning there was no causality between the senti-

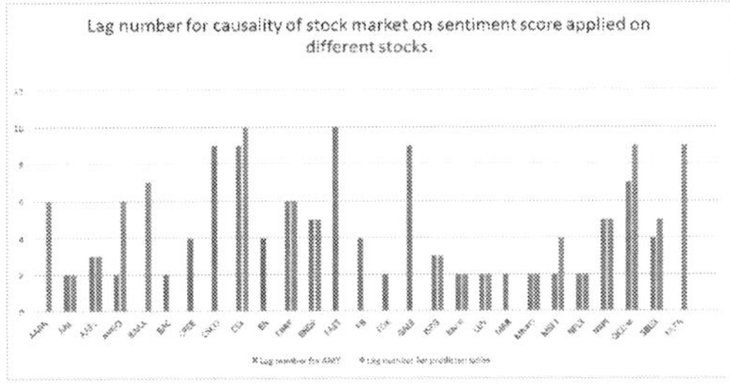

Figure 4: Lag number for GC for various stocks in model one.Lag is the number of days before current day that stock market return had causal effect on sentiment scores.

ment scores and the stock return in any lags.

Figure 4 is the plot of the lag number in which the Granger Causality model was statistically significant for different stocks in model one (impact of stock market return on sentiment results). The stocks with just one bar indicate that the causality model for the other sentiment dataset was not significant in any lags, meaning there was no causality between the sentiment dataset and the stock return in any lags. Although out of all the stocks, this model showed statistically significance for more companies, but there is less consistency shown between two sentiment dataset.

4 Evaluation

Although as long as the f-test in Granger causality is statistically significant, then the causality test is proven and done, but in order to understand this causality relationship better, we attempted to investigate certain dates in different stocks and understand the news that affected company stock on certain dates and how did it affected the Twitter which created our causality results. In the next parts, for different stocks that actually showed causality with presented analysis, we focus on specific dates. While focusing on the news that actually affected the stock, we show that there was a significant trend of that news on Twitter specially focusing the news.

4.1 Apple Inc.

According to our Granger causality model, Apple shows a lag of two days on impact of social media on stock market return. On *February first*, Apple Inc ($APPL) released [4] its profitable first quarter report which was above expectations and the

4 www.marketwatch.com

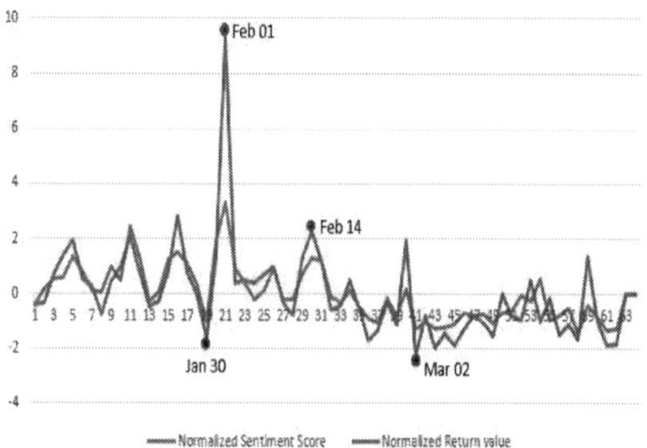

Sentiment score vs Return value plot for Apple

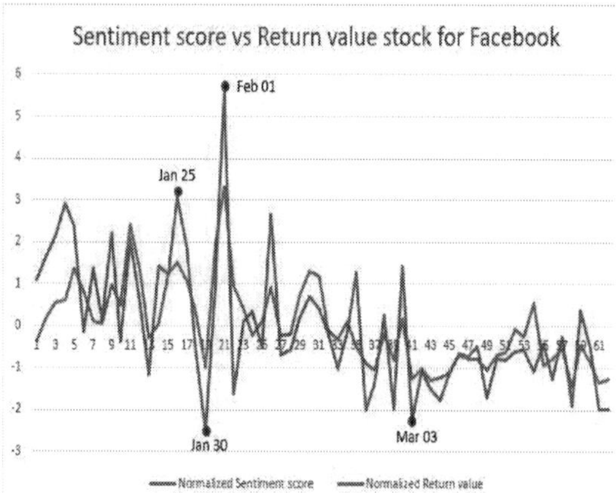

Sentiment score vs Return value stock for Facebook

Figure 5: This shows normalized tweeter sentiments calculated by Amazon Mechanical Turk and the Apple stock returns.

Figure 6: This shows normalized tweeter sentiments calculated by Amazon Mechanical Turk and the FaceBook stock returns.

Table 4: Example of Tweets targeting APPL

Date	Tweet
'stockalert stocks watch today wallstreet aapl ua'	02/01/2017
'rt igtv chinas growing faster aapl results rise copper prices theres turn around sentiment'	02/01/2017
'apple iphone sales road record quarter aapl'	02/01/2017
'apple report first numbers slew new products selling including new macbook pro iphone 7 aapl'	1/31/2017
rt optionsaction 3 stocks could account 60 billion market cap swing week aapl fb amzn'	1/31/2017

Table 5: Example of Tweets targeting FB

Date	Tweet
'facebook earnings bell wow like apple also much trump bad tech check aapl fb amzn nflx amp nasdaq ytd'	02/01/2017
'facebook rallying close hope big number think probably see good number fb earnings'	02/01/2017
'facebook deliver another record set numbers fb'	1/31/2017
'fb winning option trading facebook take via cnnmoney' '	1/31/2017

stock went up by \$4. On January 31st, Apple also reported record holiday quarter, stating iPhone7 sales boosted earnings after 3 consecutive quarters of low sales.

As it is shown in figure 5, we see a similar growth trend for the sentiment score value and the return value from January 30th to February 1st. On January 31st, Apple was set to post its numbers after the stock market closes, which created a trend of tweets regarding people suggesting to buy Apple stock on that day. There was a total of 354 tweets were sent by verified accounts on this topic, in these two dates. Table 4 shows a sample of tweets were mentioned in that two day period regarding APPL.

4.2 Facebook Inc.

Similar to Apple, the Granger causality model, shows a lag of two days on impact of social media on Facebook stock market return on figure 6. On *February first*, Facebook Inc (\$FB) reaches record territory after earnings show huge growth. [5] There was a total of 200 tweets were sent by verified accounts on this topic, in these two days. Table 5 shows a sample of tweets were mentioned in that two day period regarding FB.

5 Conclusion

In our research, on investigation on impacts of social media and stock market, we classified stock market related tweets in two different ways; using Amazon Mechanical Turk, and a classification model with accuracy of 79.9%. We then used

<hr>

[5] www.marketwatch.com

these two sentiment scores and stock market returns to understand the causality between datasets. Granger Causality analysis of these two tweet datasets with various stock returns has shown that for many companies there is a statistical significant causality between stock and the sentiments driven from tweets. At the end, investigating on the tweets sent by verified accounts in specific dates, show that when stock return has a jump due to news regarding the stock, the amount of tweets sent on Twitter jumps in the same direction, adding value to the granger causality analysis.

References

Merve Alanyali, Helen Susannah Moat, and Tobias Preis. 2013. Quantifying the relationship between financial news and the stock market. *Scientific reports*, 3:3578.

Dolan Antenucci, Michael Cafarella, Margaret C. Levenstein, Christopher Ré, and Matthew D. Shapiro. 2014. Using Social Media to Measure Labor Market Flows. *Nber*.

Johan Bollen and Alberto Pepe. 2011. Modeling Public Mood and Emotion : Twitter Sentiment and Socio-Economic Phenomena. pages 450–453.

Keith Cortis, André Freitas, Tobias Daudert, Manuela Huerlimann, Manel Zarrouk, Siegfried Handschuh, and Brian Davis. 2017. SemEval-2017 Task 5: Fine-Grained Sentiment Analysis on Financial Microblogs and News. *Proceedings of the 11th International Workshop on Semantic Evaluation (SemEval-2017)*, pages 519–535.

C W J Granger and No Aug. 1969. Investigating Causal Relations by Econometric Models and Cross-spectral Methods. 37(3):424–438.

Christopher Hitchcock. 2016. Probabilistic causation. In Edward N. Zalta, editor, *The Stanford Encyclopedia of Philosophy*, winter 2016 edition. Metaphysics Research Lab, Stanford University.

Olga Kolchyna, Tharsis T. P. Souza, Philip Treleaven, and Tomaso Aste. 2015. Twitter Sentiment Analysis: Lexicon Method, Machine Learning Method and Their Combination. page 32.

F Lillo, S Miccichè, M Tumminello, and J Piilo.... 2012. How news affect the trading behavior of different categories of investors in a financial market. *Papers.Ssrn.Com*, (April):30.

T I M Loughran and Bill Mcdonald. 2010. When is a Liability not a Liability ? Textual Analysis , Dictionaries , and 10-Ks Journal of Finance , forthcoming.

Gabriele Ranco, Darko Aleksovski, Guido Caldarelli, Miha Grčar, and Igor Mozetič. 2015. The effects of twitter sentiment on stock price returns. *PLoS ONE*, 10(9):1–21.

Rion Snow, Brendan O Connor, Daniel Jurafsky, Andrew Y Ng, Dolores Labs, and Capp St. 2008. Cheap and Fast But is it Good ? Evaluating Non-Expert Annotations for Natural Language Tasks. (October):254–263.

Thársis Tuani Pinto Souza, Olga Kolchyna, and Tomaso Aste. 2015. Twitter Sentiment Analysis Applied to Finance: A Case Study in the Retail Industry. (i):19.

Patrick Suppes. 1970. *A probabilistic theory of causality*. Amsterdam : North-Holland Pub. Co. Bibliography: p. [121]-124.

Narges Tabari, Armin Seyeditabari, and Wlodek Zadrozny. 2017. SentiHeros at SemEval-2017 Task 5 : An application of Sentiment Analysis on Financial Tweets. pages 857–860.

A   Additional Positive/Negative words

A.1   Positive words added to Loughran's list

"cover, cool, top, yes, smart, smartly, epic, highs, recover, profit, profits, long, upside, love, interesting, loved, dip, dipping, secure, longs, longput, rise, able, okay, buy, buying"

A.2   Negative words added to Loughran's list

"avoid, notokay, little, less, cray, no, crash, crashes, leaves, terrible, struggles, struggled, stall, stalls, stalled, lows, fakenews, mess, exit, not, cheaper, cheap, slaughter, slaughtered, slaughtering, disgusting, cult, brutal, fucked, suck, decay, bubble, bounce, bounced, low, lower, selloff, disgust, meltdown, downtrend, downtrends, censored, toppy, scam, censor, garbage, risk, steal, retreat, retreats, sad, dirt, flush, dump, plunge, plunged, crush, crushed, crying, unhappy, drop, dropping, drops, cry, dumped, torture, short, shorts, shorting, fall, falling, sell, selling, sells, bearish, slipping, slip, sink, sinked, sinking, pain, shortput, bullshit, shit, nervous, damn, broke, breakup, overbought"

B   List of Word-Couples

B.1   Negative Word-Couples replaced by "notokay"

(no, long), (pay, well), (no, higher), (lower, high), (terrible, market), (lose, momentum), (lost, momentum), (loses, momentum), (not, enjoy), (not, good), (lower, profit), (fall, short), (dont, trust),

(poor, sales), (not, working), (cut, pay), (cuts,
pay), (fake, news), (wasnt, great), (lost, profit),
(losses, profit), (lose, profit), (new, low), (cant,
growth), (cant, profitable), (terrible, idea), (short,
sellers), (raises, concern), (raise, concern), (not,
recommend), (not, recommended), (not, much),
(big, debt), (high, down), (lipstick, pig), (doesnt,
well), (bounce, buy), (isnt, cheap), (fear, sell),
(cant, down), (not, good), (wont, buy), (dont,
trade), (buy, back), (didnt, like), (profit, exit),
(go, down), (not , guaranteed), (not, profitable),
(doesn't, upward), (not, dip), (pull, back), (not,
optimistic), (go, up, okay), (not, affected, okay),
(not, concerned, okay), (short, trap, okay), (exit,
short, okay), (sell, exhaust, okay), (didnt, stop,
okay), (short, cover, okay), (close, short, okay),
(short, break, okay), (cant, risk, okay), (not, sell,
okay), (dont, fall, okay), (sold, call, okay), (dont,
short, okay), (exit, bancruptsy, okay), (not, bad,
okay), (short, nervous, okay), (dont, underesti-
mate, okay), (not, slowdown, okay), (aint, bad,
okay), (first, second, replacement)

B.2 Positive Word-Couples replaced by "okay"

(go, up), (not, affected), (not, concerned), (short,
trap), (exit, short), (sell, exhaust), (didnt, stop),
(short, cover), (close, short), (short, break), (cant,
risk), (not, sell), (dont, fall), (sold, call), (dont,
short), (exit, bancruptsy), (not, bad), (short, nervous), (dont, understimate), (not, slowdown),
(aint, bad)

C Results of Granger Causality

C.1 F-test and P-value for Model 1

Stock Symbol	AMT Lag number	F-value	P-value	ML Lag number	F-value	P-value
AABA	Not Significant			6	2.76	0.023
AAL	2	3.99	0.024	2	4.2	0.02
AAPL	3	4.23	0.01	3	5.68	0.002
AVGO	2	3.85	0.027	6	2.87	0.02
BABA	Not Significant			7	2.86	0.016
BAC	2	3.44	0.039	Not Significant		
CREE	4	3.11	0.024	Not Significant		
CSCO	9	2.55	0.024	Not Significant		
CSX	9	2.47	0.028	Not Significant	2.17	0.049
EA	4	3.13	0.023	Not Significant		
EBAY	6	2.39	0.045	6	2.33	0.05
ENDP	5	2.53	0.042	5	2.7	0.032
FAST	10	2.28	0.039	Not Significant		
FB	4	2.84	0.034	Not Significant		
FDX	2	3.41	0.04	Not Significant		
GALE	9	2.47	0.028	Not Significant		
ISRG	3	6.31	0.001	3	4.01	0.012
KNDI	2	3.71	0.031	2	3.81	0.028
LUV	2	3.93	0.025	2	2.23	0.117
MAR	2	3.49	0.038	Not Significant		
MNKD	2	3.75	0.03	2	3.57	0.035
MSFT	2	3.8	0.029	4	2.94	0.03
NFLX	2	4.64	0.014	2	4.16	0.021
NXPI	5	3.93	0.005	5	3.12	0.017
QCOM	7	2.6	0.027	9	2.31	0.038
SBUX	4	2.7	0.042	5	2.35	0.048
ULTA	Not Significant			9	2.22	0.046

C.2 F-test and P-value for Model 2

Stock Symbol	AMT Lag number	F-value	P-value	ML Lag number	F-value	P-value
AAPL	2	5.86	0.005	2	3.98	0.024
AGN	4	2.65	0.045	4	3.10	0.024
AMZN	3	2.93	0.042	3	3.01	0.038
BABA	6	2.61	0.03	Not significant		
CELG	10	2.57	0.022	10	2.58	0.022
COST	2	4.16	0.021	2	3.89	0.026
CSCO	Not significant			2	3.59	0.034
FB	2	3.83	0.028	2	4.31	0.018
FFIV	Not significant			3	2.95	0.041
GALE	4	3.65	0.011	4	4.14	0.006
GILD	6	2.72	0.025	6	2.54	0.035
MSFT	5	3.06	0.018	5	2.50	0.044
PLUG	10	2.37	0.033	10	2.19	0.047
REGN	7	2.45	0.035	6	2.38	0.046
SINA	5	2.5	0.044	Not significant		
STX	Not significant			3	2.98	0.040
TWTR	5	3.81	0.006	5	4.89	0.001
YELP	2	3.34	0.043	6	3.07	0.014
ZNGA	Not significant			6	2.53	0.035

A Corpus of Corporate Annual and Social Responsibility Reports: 280 Million Tokens of Balanced Organizational Writing

Sebastian G. M. Händschke[2] *   Sven Buechel[1] *   Jan Goldenstein[2]

Philipp Poschmann[2]   Tinghui Duan[1]   Peter Walgenbach[2]   Udo Hahn[1]

[1] Jena University Language and Information Engineering (JULIE) Lab
http://www.julielab.de

[2] School of Economics and Business Administration
http://www.orga.uni-jena.de

Friedrich-Schiller-Universität Jena, Jena, Germany

Abstract

We introduce JOCo, a novel text corpus for NLP analytics in the field of economics, business and management. This corpus is composed of corporate annual and social responsibility reports of the top 30 US, UK and German companies in the major (DJIA, FTSE 100, DAX), middle-sized (S&P 500, FTSE 250, MDAX) and technology (NASDAQ, FTSE AIM 100, TECDAX) stock indices, respectively. Altogether, this adds up to 5,000 reports from 270 companies headquartered in three of the world's most important economies. The corpus spans a time frame from 2000 up to 2015 and contains, in total, 282M tokens. We also feature JOCo in a small-scale experiment to demonstrate its potential for NLP-fueled studies in economics, business and management research.

1   Introduction

A crucial prerequisite in today's NLP research is the availability of large amounts of language data. National reference corpora such as the ANC for American English (Ide and Suderman, 2004), the BNC for British English (Burnard, 2000), and the DEREKo for German (Kupietz and Lüngen, 2014) assemble a collection of language data with a focus on ordinary language use covering a wide range of genres (e.g., newspaper articles, technical writing and popular fiction, letters, transcripts of court or parliament speeches, etc.). Corpora exclusively focusing on newspaper articles have been particularly influential for the development of syntactic and semantic methodologies in NLP

research (e.g., PENN TREEBANK (Marcus et al., 1993) or PENN PROPBANK (Palmer et al., 2005) for the English language).

Turning to more specialized, mostly scientific, domains these general language resources can only be reused at the cost of substantial performance penalties due to characteristic sublanguage phenomena in those domains. For the biomedical domain, e.g., these negative effects can be shown for the whole range of low-level (sentence splitting, tokenization (Tomanek et al., 2007; Griffis et al., 2016)) up to high-level tasks (such as syntactic analysis (Laippala et al., 2014; Jiang et al., 2015)). As a consequence, these specialized fields of NLP research have created their own resource infrastructure in terms of domain-specific lexicons and corpora for syntactic and semantic processing.

The rapidly increasing number of publications using text analytics for economics, business, and management (for surveys, cf. Lu et al. (2010); Goldenstein et al. (2015); Kumar and Ravi (2016)) indicates the emergence of an entirely new application domain for NLP systems (see Section 2). At first sight, one might argue that domain-specific corpora such as the PENN TREEBANK are sufficient since they already contain economy-related language data. Yet, as these resources assemble only excerpts from newspaper articles, at second sight, such resources turn out to be biased. Newspaper articles reflect *journalists'* interpretations and do not necessarily directly transport the attitudes and views of *economic actors*, such as an individual (consumer) or business corporations (Simon, 1991).

This shortcoming can be alleviated if one targets the economic actors' verbal communication behavior directly on various media channels. Our choice is to focus on annual reports (AR) and corporate social responsibility reports (CSRR) of major business corporations in Western economies.

---

* These authors contributed equally to this work.

Proceedings of the First Workshop on Economics and Natural Language Processing, pages 20–31
Melbourne, Australia, July 20, 2018. ©2018 Association for Computational Linguistics

Altogether these documents comprise 282M tokens and reflect the unfiltered views of these commercial enterprises *and* their embedding in the social and regulatory system in market-driven societies. Viewing enterprises as social actors with their own goals, their legal, social and other responsibilities becomes increasingly relevant for both the explanation and prediction of economic and organizational phenomena, as well as for economics, management and organization science, in general (King et al., 2010; Bromley and Sharkey, 2017). While the raw data set we assembled can be used for scientific purposes only, we also offer an embedding model trained on it which is available without any legal restrictions.[1]

2 Related Work

The ties between NLP, economics, management, and organization science have evolved around different types of economic actors and roles they play in an economic setting. One stream of work deals with NLP-based *customer* analytics by profiling customers, tracking their product/company preferences, screening customer reviews, etc. (Archak et al., 2011; Ikeda et al., 2013; Zhang and Pennacchiotti, 2013; Stavrianou and Brun, 2015; Yang et al., 2015; Sakaki et al., 2016; Pekar and Binner, 2017). Another stream is concerned with NLP-based *product* analytics, e.g., based on (social) media monitoring, summarizing reviews, or identifying (deceptive/fake) product descriptions or reviews (Mukherjee et al., 2012; Feng et al., 2012; Wang and Ester, 2014; Tsunoda et al., 2015; Fang and Zhan, 2015; Kessler et al., 2015; Imada et al., 2016; Chen et al., 2016; Pryzant et al., 2017).

Yet, the main thrust of work is devoted to NLP-based financial *(stock) market* analytics, e.g., analyzing companies' market performance indicators (trend prediction, performance forecasting, volatility prediction, etc.) and verbal statements related to market performance, competitors or future perspectives (Schumaker and Chen, 2009; Kogan et al., 2009; Nassirtoussi et al., 2014; Li et al., 2014; Qiu and Srinivasan, 2014; Kazemian et al., 2014; de Fortuny et al., 2014; Ammann et al., 2014; Wang and Hua, 2014; Nguyen and Shirai, 2015; Luss and d'Aspremont, 2015; Ding et al., 2015; Liu et al., 2015; Feuerriegel and Prendinger, 2016; Rekabsaz et al., 2017; Xing et al., 2018; Li et al., 2018).

This external market view is complemented by NLP-based *organization/enterprise* analytics, e.g., social role taking, risk prediction, fraud analysis, market share analytics, etc. (Goel et al., 2010; Hájek and Olej, 2015; Buechel et al., 2016; Goel and Uzuner, 2016; El-Haj et al., 2016; Tsai and Wang, 2017), including *competitive* or *business intelligence* services based on NLP tooling (Chaudhuri et al., 2011; Chung, 2014).

From a methodological perspective, the social interactions between these actors—customers, enterprises, and political/juridical authorities—have been studied in terms of *sentiments* they bring to bear (Van De Kauter et al., 2015). Evidence is collected from consumers' and enterprises' verbal behavior and their communication about products and services, e.g., via social media (Chen et al., 2014; Si et al., 2014; Liu, 2015; Alshahrani et al., 2018). This research is complemented by studies related to *reputation, expertise, credibility and trust* models for agents in the economic process (as traders, sellers, advertisers) based on mining communication traces and recommendation legacy data, including fake ad/review recognition (Bar-Haim et al., 2011; Brown, 2012; Mukherjee et al., 2012; Rechenthin et al., 2013; Tang and Chen, 2014; Žnidaršič et al., 2018).

System-wise, specialized types of search engines have been developed, for instance, *enterprise search engines* (e-commerce, e-marketing) or *consumer search engines*, market monitors, product/service recommender systems (Vandic et al., 2017; Trotman et al., 2017). This also includes *customer-supplier interaction platforms* (e.g., portals, helps desks, newsgroups) and transaction support systems based on natural language communication (including business chat bots) (Cui et al., 2017; Altinok, 2018). Specialized modes of *information extraction* and text mining in economic domains, e.g., temporal event or transaction mining have also been explored (Tao et al., 2015; Lefever and Hoste, 2016; Ding et al., 2016), as well as *information aggregation* from single sources (e.g., review summaries, automatic threading) (Gerani et al., 2014).

The language resources behind these activities include specialized *lexicons* (Loughran and McDonald, 2011) and *ontologies* for economics (Leibniz Information Centre for Economics, 2014), the adaptation or acquisition of lexicons

[1] `www.orga.uni-jena.de/orga/en/Corpus.html` for economic NLP (Xie et al., 2013; Moore et al.,

2016; Oliveira et al., 2016; Chen et al., 2018), *corpora* and annotations policies (guidelines, metadata schemata, etc.) for economic NLP concerned with domain-specific text genres (business reports, auditing documents, product reviews, economic newswire, social media posts or blogs, business letters, legislation documents, etc.) (Flickinger et al., 2012; Takala et al., 2014; Kessler and Kuhn, 2014; Asooja et al., 2015; Schön et al., 2018) , and dedicated *tools* for economic NLP (e.g., NER taggers, sublanguage parsers, pipelines for processing economic discourse) (Schumaker and Chen, 2009; Feldman et al., 2011; Hogenboom et al., 2013; Kessler and Kuhn, 2013; Lee et al., 2014; Malo et al., 2014; Weichselbraun et al., 2015; Lefever and Hoste, 2016; Ding et al., 2016; El-Haj et al., 2018).

Pioneering efforts in considering texts originally produced by enterprises as a basis for economic NLP were made by Kloptchenko et al. (2004) who used sentiments in enterprises' quarterly reports as a predictor for stock market prices. Later Kogan et al. (2009) came up with the influential *10-K Corpus*, a collection of 54,379 ARs from 10,492 different, publically traded companies covering a time interval from 1996 up to 2006. This seminal resource is a cornerstone of economic corpus development and our work is meant to complement it with current and more diverse language data.

3 Corpus Description

The corpus we here introduce consists of ARs and CSRRs from companies in the United States, the United Kingdom and Germany. An *AR* is a comprehensive report published yearly by publicly-listed corporations on their activities and financial performance of the past year. ARs provide information for current and prospective shareholders, the governmental and regulatory bodies, the stock exchanges, as well as all other stakeholders (Neu et al., 1998; Yuthas et al., 2002). A *CSRR* is a regular report published by a company or an organization about the economic, environmental and social impacts caused by its activities (Dahlsrud, 2008; Chen and Bouvain, 2009; Fifka, 2013). CSRRs also present the organization's values and governance model, and reveal the link between its strategy and its commitment to the organization's environment and a sustainable global economy (Du et al., 2010; Aguinis and Glavas, 2012).

With regard to the popular 10-K corpus (Kogan et al., 2009), the data set we present is significantly smaller in size (both in terms of tokens and companies). However, the 10-K corpus only covers ARs, while we also include CSRRs allowing a wider view on organizational communication traces. Also, the 10-K corpus only includes reports up to the year 2006, whereas our work incorporates documents as recent as 2015. Additionally, the 10-K corpus is only based on the 10-k forms mandated by the Securities Exchange Commission (SEC) in the US. Nonetheless, US corporations' ARs contain the same information as required by the 10-k forms and much more. Furthermore, ARs are a genre of reports diffused globally (Rutherford, 2005; Meyer and Höllerer, 2010). Hence, the choice of ARs as a backbone for our corpus allows for a careful international sampling strategy balancing different kinds of corporations from different countries. This property makes our corpus particularly well suited for deeper economic investigations with respect to cross-index, cross-industry and cross-country comparisons.

3.1 Selection of Raw Data

ARs as well as CSRRs are considered relevant for our corpus based on two main criteria, namely the company that issued them and the year they report about. We selected companies in a step-wise process, first selecting the countries of origin and then the stock indices they were listed in.

Regarding the selection of countries, we chose the US, the UK and Germany, because altogether their total GDP makes up for 30% of the WGDP (as of 2014), thus representing a relevant portion of the global economy. For each of these three countries, 90 companies where selected for inclusion in our corpus. We first took the 30 most intensively traded and most highly valued corporations of the American Dow Jones Industrial Average (DIJA), the British Financial Times Stock Exchange (FTSE 100) and the German Stock Index (DAX; "Deutscher Aktienindex"). Next, we added reports of middle-sized companies (30 per country) and technology companies (again 30 per country) for a total of 270 companies in our sample. Middle-sized companies were selected from the S&P500, the FTSE 250 and the MDAX, whereas tech firms were chosen from the NASDAQ, the FTSE AIM 100 and the TECDAX indices for the US, the UK and Germany, respectively. We se-

Index	Annual Reports			Corporate Social Responsibility Reps			Total		
	Tokens	Sentences	Reps	Tokens	Sentences	Reps	Tokens	Sentences	Reps
DIJA	27,139,371	864,724	458	7,168,558	253,564	239	34,307,929	1,118,288	697
S&P500	23,914,717	780,372	335	2,902,234	101,707	113	26,816,951	882,079	448
NASDAQ	24,937,589	737,156	342	896,070	32,769	58	25,833,659	769,925	400
FTSE 100	47,086,382	1,458,637	452	8,913,870	322,565	278	56,000,252	1,781,202	730
FTSE 250	20,654,093	619,239	472	1,657,327	56,052	86	22,311,420	675,291	558
FTSE AIM 100	15,878,972	477,245	426	207,220	7,746	30	16,086,192	484,991	456
DAX	45,170,200	1,535,016	469	9,646,971	362,162	254	54,817,171	1,897,178	723
MDAX	23,198,101	786,189	366	3,193,350	116,437	93	26,391,451	902,626	459
TechDAX	19,083,290	654,875	350	203,393	8,076	15	19,286,683	662,951	365
Total	247,062,715	7,913,453	3,670	34,788,993	1,261,078	1,166	281,851,708	9,174,531	4,836

Table 1: Numbers of tokens, sentences and reports relative to stock index and report category.

economy		*growth*		*tax*		*leadership*		*sustainable*	
recession	.70	grow	.66	taxes	.73	leaders	.66	sustainably	.64
economies	.69	double-digit	.64	taxation	.71	excellence	.57	sustainability	.64
upswing	.68	strong	.63	deferred	.65	reinforce	.56	environmentally	.56
upturn	.67	organic	.60	non-deductible	.61	leader	.55	stewardship	.56
gdp	.66	profitable	.60	carryforwards	.57	competencies	.55	low-carbon	.54

Table 2: Sample word embeddings illustrated by their five nearest neighbors based on cosine similarity.

lected each corporation from the three countries so that they matched the corresponding two counterparts with respect to industry segment, sales and trading volumes.

Lastly, we let the time span of our corpus range between the years 2000 and 2015. Each report (AR and CSRR) from one of the 270 companies in the previously defined sample that addresses one of these years was included in the corpus, if possible (see also the following Subsection 3.2). The year 2000 was chosen as a starting point because of, first, the burst of the dotcom-bubble and, second, the upcoming of CSRRs. Further details regarding our sampling strategy are provided in the README file of our corpus distribution.

3.2 Data Acquisition and Cleansing

The reports determined in this way were collected by three student assistants from the Business and Management Department by downloading the reports in PDF format from the companies' websites. In some cases, especially for documents from the early 2000s, reports were not available for downloading. The students (and, if necessary, one of the authors) then requested the documents directly from the respective investor relations department via email. The following metadata were recorded: *report type* (either AR or CSRR), *reference year* of the report[2] (as given on the title page), *company* of origin, and *stock index*.

<hr>

[2] In some cases, and in particular with regard to CSRR, sometimes multiple consecutive years were indicated. In these cases, only the first year is considered as reference year.

We used the pdf2text software by `glyphand-cog.com` to extract plain text from the collected PDF files. In general, this software extracts text with sufficient quality. However, the final result depends heavily on the layout and style of the input files. For this reason, the resulting plain text files were iteratively refined in a rule-based fashion. This post-processing included restoring of the original text structure of headings and paragraphs, deleting superfluous line breaks and hyphenation, page numbers and (rarely occurring) odd character sequences, as well as remnants of structured data, such as tables. This post-processing strategy yielded a mostly clean corpus of raw textual data only, i.e., preserving the running text of the original PDF files as good as possible while at the same time stripping off all irrelevant non-linguistic data.

3.3 Corpus Analysis

After corpus construction, we used `NLTK.org` tools (Bird, 2006) for counting tokens and sentences for all of the reports. The results, summarized for each stock index, are depicted in Table 1. In total, our corpus comprises almost 5,000 reports, summing up to 282M tokens (9M sentences). This constitutes a substantial collection of textual data (for comparison, the BNC, ANC, and DEREKO contain 100M, 15M, and 42B tokens, respectively). The vast majority of the data set consists of ARs (247M tokens vs. 35M tokens from CSRRs). American, British and German corporations are properly represented in the data set,

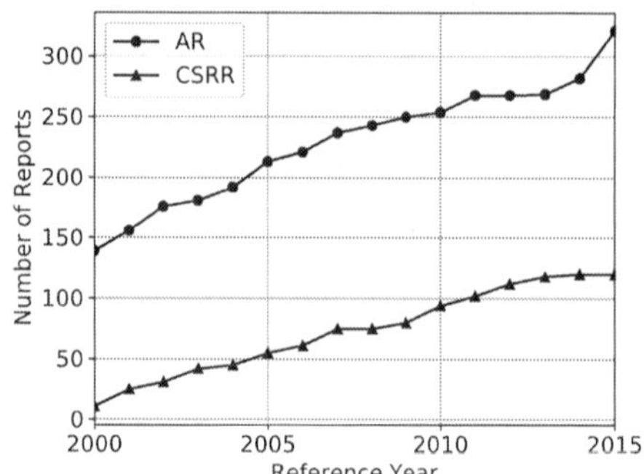

Figure 1: Distribution of reports over time.

i.e., for each of these countries, their three indices add up to about 90M tokens.

Figure 1 depicts the growth curves for ARs as well as CSRRs. As can be seen, for both ARs and CSRRs, the number of reports increases over time. This graph also reflects the fact that documents become harder to acquire the older they are, as we have experienced during data collection. Note that we could only collect a marginal number of CSRRs for the year 2000 (11). This is due to the fact, that their issuance became wide-spread only in this and the following years, as discussed above.

3.4 Word Embeddings

The distribution of the plain text data of JOCo is restricted by Intellectual Property Rights (IPR) regulations. As a substitute, we train word embeddings using the `FastText.cc` toolkit (Bojanowski et al., 2017) to capture the distributional semantics of economic jargon. As a prerequisite, the corpus was tokenized using NLTK and case-folded. Only words with frequency ≥ 50 were modeled. Subword information was *not* taken into account. The latter two decision were taken to decrease the number of artifacts stemming from the PDF conversion in our final embedding model.

To illustrate the semantics captured in this way, Table 2 lists sample entries of our embedding model together with their five nearest neighbors. As can be seen, the results reveal high face validity: *"growth"*, e.g., exhibits strong reference to its economic meaning (such as in *"double-digit growth"* or *"organic growth"*) but does not refer to biological growth which may have been indicated by neighbors like *"plant"* or *"hormones"*.

4 Effects of Organizational Emotions

To demonstrate the potential of the JOCo corpus, we investigate the interaction of linguistic signals from corporations and their market performance. We focus on emotions expressed in ARs since the interplay of organizational cognition, character, and emotions is becoming a hot topic in organization science (Albrow, 1992; King, 2015; Buechel et al., 2016; Händschke et al., 2017). We conducted this work on a subsample of the corpus covering British and German firms only and their ARs from 2008 to 2015 to allow for European comparability. Financial and accounting metadata were retrieved from AMADEUS,[3] a database that holds data of European firms (except for banks and insurance companies).

In the regression analysis, we employ the generalized estimating equations (GEE) method (Liang and Zeger, 1986), a time series model that handles repeating observations over time. In our case we use its multivariate linear regression variant (see the Appendix for details). The dependent variable 'performance' is operationalized as *Return on Equity (ROE)*, lagged by one year to allow for causality. Following the established psychological VAD model of emotions (Bradley and Lang, 1994), the independent explanatory variables are three dimensions of espoused organizational emotions—*Valence*, *Arousal*, and *Dominance*. These three dimensions are measured individually for each AR using the open-source tool JEmAS[4] (Buechel and Hahn, 2016) that yields a value for each of the dimensions per firm per year. Due to the high correlation between dominance and valence, the latter variable was dropped from the model to prevent biasing of the estimators (cf. the correlation matrix given in the Appendix, Table 3). Control variables are the corporation's size (in terms of employees and assets, both logarithmized),[5] operational profitability (sales per employee and sales per assets) and country of origin measured with a dummy variable where Germany is coded as '1'.

For our full model (Model III in Table 4), we find that Arousal has a significant ($p < .001$) negative effect on ROE, meaning that a company performs better, the calmer it communicates. However, this effect is more pronounced for British companies since the interaction term be-

---

[3] `https://amadeus.bvdinfo.com/`
[4] `https://github.com/JULIELab/JEmAS`
[5] All other metric variables have been standardized.

tween Arousal and country (GER) shows a significant ($p < .001$) positive effect. Thus, our results suggest that espoused organizational emotionality correlates with performance, yet the nature of this interaction is country-dependent. Accordingly, our findings point towards the existence of a distinct organizational character (King, 2015) and emotionality (Albrow, 1992), and thus render support viewing organizations as social actors (King et al., 2010; Bromley and Sharkey, 2017). This piece of evidence might have far-reaching implications for the organizations' role and responsibility in society (Beyer et al., 2014).

5 Conclusion

We introduced JOCo, a novel text corpus for NLP analytics in the field of economics, business and management. This corpus comprises ARs and CSRRs of 270 publicly traded corporations in the US, UK and Germany from 2000 to 2015. Altogether, we assembled roughly up to 5,000 reports and, in total, 282M tokens (9M sentences). By design, JOCo carefully balances various characteristics allowing cross-index, cross-industry, and cross-country comparisons and, thus, enables informed prospective applications in business research and economics, for which we provided a first, yet preliminary example.

Acknowledgments

We thank the anonymous reviewers for their helpful comments, as well as our research assistants, esp. Nadine Halli, for their effort in assembling the primary documents.

References

Herman Aguinis and Ante Glavas. 2012. What we know and don't know about corporate social responsibility: A review and research agenda. *Journal of Management*, 38(4):932–968.

Martin Albrow. 1992. Sine ira et studio—or do organizations have feelings? *Organization Studies*, 13(3):313–329.

Mohammed Alshahrani, Fuxi Zhu, Mohammed Alghaili, Eshrag Refaee, and Mervat Bamiah. 2018. BORSAH: An Arabic sentiment financial tweets corpus. In *FNP 2018 — Proceedings of the 1st Financial Narrative Processing Workshop @ LREC 2018. Miyazaki, Japan, 7 May 2018*, pages 17–22.

Duygu Altinok. 2018. An ontology-based dialogue management system for banking and finance dialogue systems. In *FNP 2018 — Proceedings of the 1st Financial Narrative Processing Workshop @ LREC 2018. Miyazaki, Japan, 7 May 2018*, pages 1–9.

Manuel Ammann, Roman Frey, and Michael Verhofen. 2014. Do newspaper articles predict aggregate stock returns? *Journal of Behavioral Finance*, 15(3):195–213.

Nikolay Archak, Anindya Ghose, and Panagiotis G. Ipeirotis. 2011. Deriving the pricing power of product features by mining consumer reviews. *Management Science*, 57(8):1485–1509.

Kartik Asooja, Georgeta Bordea, Gabriela Vulcu, Leona O'Brien, Angelina Espinoza, Elie Abi-Lahoud, Paul Buitelaar, and Tom Butler. 2015. Semantic annotation of finance regulatory text using multilabel classification. In *LeDA-SWAn 2015 — Proceedings of the 2015 International Workshop on Legal Domain and Semantic Web Applications @ ESWC 2015. Portorož, Slovenia, June 1, 2015.*

Roy Bar-Haim, Elad Dinur, Ronen Feldman, Moshe Fresko, and Guy Goldstein. 2011. Identifying and following expert investors in stock microblogs. In *EMNLP 2011 — Proceedings of the 2011 Conference on Empirical Methods in Natural Language Processing. Edinburgh, Scotland, U.K., 27-31 July 2011*, pages 1310–1319.

Susan Beyer, Stephan Bohn, Toni Grünheid, Sebastian Händschke, Raluca Kerekes, Jonas Müller, and Peter Walgenbach. 2014. Wofür übernehmen Unternehmungen Verantwortung? Und wie kommunizieren sie ihre Verantwortungsübernahme? *Zeitschrift für Wirtschafts- und Unternehmensethik*, 15(1):57–80.

Steven Bird. 2006. NLTK: The Natural Language Toolkit. In *COLING-ACL 2006 — Proceedings of the 21st International Conference on Computational Linguistics & 44th Annual Meeting of the Association for Computational Linguistics: Interactive Presentation Sessions. Sydney, New South Wales, Australia, 17-18 July 2006*, pages 69–72.

Piotr Bojanowski, Edouard Grave, Armand Joulin, and Tomáš Mikolov. 2017. Enriching word vectors with subword information. *Transactions of the Association for Computational Linguistics*, 5(1):135–146.

Margaret M. Bradley and Peter J. Lang. 1994. Measuring emotion: The Self-Assessment Manikin and the semantic differential. *Journal of Behavior Therapy and Experimental Psychiatry*, 25(1):49–59.

Patricia Bromley and Amanda Sharkey. 2017. Casting call: The expanding nature of actorhood in US firms, 1960–2010. *Accounting, Organizations and Society*, 59:3–20.

Eric D. Brown. 2012. Will Twitter make you a better investor? A look at sentiment, user reputation and their effect on the stock market. In *SAIS 2012 —*

Proceedings of the Southern Association for Information Systems Conference. Atlanta, Georgia, USA, March 23-24, 2012, pages 36–42.

Sven Buechel and Udo Hahn. 2016. Emotion analysis as a regression problem: Dimensional models and their implications on emotion representation and metrical evaluation. In *ECAI 2016 — Proceedings of the 22nd European Conference on Artificial Intelligence. Including Prestigious Applications of Artificial Intelligence (PAIS 2016). The Hague, The Netherlands, August 29 - September 2, 2016*, number 285 in Frontiers in Artificial Intelligence and Applications, pages 1114–1122, Amsterdam, Berlin, Washington, D.C. IOS Press.

Sven Buechel, Udo Hahn, Jan Goldenstein, Sebastian G. M. Händschke, and Peter Walgenbach. 2016. Do enterprises have emotions? In *WASSA 2016 — Proceedings of the 7th Workshop on Computational Approaches to Subjectivity, Sentiment and Social Media Analysis @ NAACL-HLT 2016. San Diego, California, USA, June 16, 2016*, pages 147–153.

Lou Burnard. 2000. User Reference Guide for the British National Corpus. Technical report, British National Corpus Consortium, Humanities Computing Unit, Oxford University Computing Services, Oxford University, Oxford, U.K.

Surajit Chaudhuri, Umeshwar Dayal, and Vivek Narasayya. 2011. An overview of business intelligence technology. *Communications of the ACM*, 54(8):88–98.

Chung-Chi Chen, Hen-Hsen Huang, and Hsin-Hsi Chen. 2018. NTUSD-FIN: A market sentiment dictionary for financial social media data applications. In *FNP 2018 — Proceedings of the 1st Financial Narrative Processing Workshop @ LREC 2018. Miyazaki, Japan, 7 May 2018*, pages 37–43.

Hailiang Chen, Prabuddha De, Yu (Jeffrey) Hu, and Byoung-Hyoun Hwang. 2014. Wisdom of crowds: The value of stock opinions transmitted through social media. *The Review of Financial Studies*, 27(5):1367–1403.

Huimin Chen, Maosong Sun, Cunchao Tu, Yankai Lin, and Zhiyuan Liu. 2016. Neural sentiment classification with user and product attention. In *EMNLP 2016 — Proceedings of the 2016 Conference on Empirical Methods in Natural Language Processing. Austin, Texas, USA, November 1-5, 2016*, pages 1650–1659.

Stephen Chen and Petra Bouvain. 2009. Is corporate responsibility converging? A comparison of corporate responsibility reporting in the USA, UK, Australia, and Germany. *Journal of Business Ethics*, 87(1):299–317.

Wingyan Chung. 2014. BIZPRO: Extracting and categorizing business intelligence factors from textual news articles. *International Journal of Information Management*, 34(2):272–284.

Lei Cui, Shaohan Huang, Furu Wei, Chuanqi Tan, Chaoqun Duan, and Ming Zhou. 2017. SUPER-AGENT: A customer service chatbot for e-commerce websites. In *ACL 2017 — Proceedings of the 55th Annual Meeting of the Association for Computational Linguistics: System Demonstrations. Vancouver, British Columbia, Canada, August 1, 2017*, pages 97–102.

Alexander Dahlsrud. 2008. How corporate social responsibility is defined: An analysis of 37 definitions. *Corporate Social Responsibility and Environmental Management*, 15(1):1–13.

Xiao Ding, Yue Zhang, Ting Liu, and Junwen Duan. 2015. Deep learning for event-driven stock prediction. In *IJCAI '15 — Proceedings of the 24th International Joint Conference on Artificial Intelligence. Buenos Aires, Argentina, July 25-31, 2015*, pages 2327–2333.

Xiao Ding, Yue Zhang, Ting Liu, and Junwen Duan. 2016. Knowledge-driven event embedding for stock prediction. In *COLING 2016 — Proceedings of the 26th International Conference on Computational Linguistics: Technical Papers. Osaka, Japan, December 11-16, 2016*, pages 2133–2142.

Shuili Du, Chitrabhan B Bhattacharya, and Sankar Sen. 2010. Maximizing business returns to corporate social responsibility (CSR): The role of CSR communication. *International Journal of Management Reviews*, 12(1):8–19.

The Leibniz Information Centre for Economics. 2014. STW thesaurus for economics. Technical report.

Mahmoud El-Haj, Paul Rayson, Paulo Alves, and Steven Young. 2018. Towards a multilingual financial narrative processing system. In *FNP 2018 — Proceedings of the 1st Financial Narrative Processing Workshop @ LREC 2018. Miyazaki, Japan, 7 May 2018*, pages 52–58.

Mahmoud El-Haj, Paul Rayson, Steven Young, Andrew Moore, Martin Walker, Thomas Schleicher, and Vasiliki Athanasakou. 2016. Learning tone and attribution for financial text mining. In *LREC 2016 — Proceedings of the 10th International Conference on Language Resources and Evaluation. Portorož, Slovenia, 23-28 May 2016*, pages 1820–1825.

Xing Fang and Justin Zhan. 2015. Sentiment analysis using product review data. *Journal of Big Data*, 2:#5.

Ronen Feldman, Benjamin Rosenfeld, Roy Bar-Haim, and Moshe Fresko. 2011. The STOCK SONAR: Sentiment analysis of stocks based on a hybrid approach. In *AAAI-IAAI-EAAI '11 — Proceedings of the 25th AAAI Conference on Artificial Intelligence & 23rd Conference on Innovative Applications of Artificial Intelligence & 2nd Symposium on Educational Advances in Artificial Intelligence. San Francisco, California, USA, August 7-11, 2011*, pages 1642–1647.

Song Feng, Longfei Xing, Anupam Gogar, and Yejin Choi. 2012. Distributional footprints of deceptive product reviews. In *ICWSM 2012 — Proceedings of the 6th International AAAI Conference on Weblogs and Social Media. Dublin, Ireland, June 4-7, 2012*, pages 98–105.

Stefan Feuerriegel and Helmut Prendinger. 2016. News-based trading strategies. *Decision Support Systems*, 90:65–74.

Matthias S. Fifka. 2013. Corporate responsibility reporting and its determinants in comparative perspective. A review of the empirical literature and a meta-analysis. *Business Strategy and the Environment*, 22(1):1–35.

Daniel P. Flickinger, Yi Zhang, and Valia Kordoni. 2012. DEEPBANK: A dynamically annotated treebank of the Wall Street Journal. In *TLT '11 — Proceedings of the 11th International Workshop on Treebanks and Linguistic Theories. Lisbon, Portugal, 30 November - 1 December 2012*, pages 85–96.

Enric Junqué de Fortuny, Tom De Smedt, David Martens, and Walter Daelemans. 2014. Evaluating and understanding text-based stock price prediction models. *Information Processing & Management*, 50(2):426–441.

Shima Gerani, Yashar Mehdad, Giuseppe Carenini, Raymond T. Ng, and Bita Nejat. 2014. Abstractive summarization of product reviews using discourse structure. In *EMNLP 2014 — Proceedings of the 2014 Conference on Empirical Methods in Natural Language Processing. Doha, Qatar, October 25-29, 2014*, pages 1602–1613.

Sunita Goel, Jagdish Gangolly, Sue R. Faerman, and Özlem Uzuner. 2010. Can linguistic predictors detect fraudulent financial filings? *Journal of Emerging Technologies in Accounting*, 7:25–46.

Sunita Goel and Özlem Uzuner. 2016. Do sentiments matter in fraud detection? Estimating semantic orientation of annual reports. *Intelligent Systems in Accounting, Finance and Management*, 23(3):215–239.

Jan Goldenstein, Philipp Poschmann, and Sebastian G. M. Händschke. 2015. Linguistic analysis: The study of textual data in management and organization studies with NLP. In *Academy of Management Proceedings*, volume 2015, page 10882. Academy of Management, Briarcliff Manor, NY.

Denis Griffis, Chaitanya Shivade, Eric Fosler-Lussier, and Albert M. Lai. 2016. A quantitative and qualitative evaluation of sentence boundary detection for the clinical domain. In *Proceedings of the AMIA 2016 Joint Summits on Translational Science. San Francisco, California, USA, March 21-24, 2016*, pages 88–97.

Petr Hájek and Vladimír Olej. 2015. Word categorization of corporate annual reports for bankruptcy prediction by machine learning methods. In *Text, Speech, and Dialogue. TSD 2015 — Proceedings of the 18th International Conference on Text, Speech, and Dialogue. Pilsen, Czech Republic, September 14-17, 2015*, number 9302 in Lecture Notes in Computer Science (LNCS), pages 122–130, Berlin. Springer.

Sebastian GM Händschke, Jan Goldenstein, and Peter Walgenbach. 2017. Cognitive isomorphism: Effects of management ideas as filters of organizational cognition. In *Academy of Management Proceedings*, volume 2017, page 14435. Academy of Management, Briarcliff Manor, NY.

Alexander Hogenboom, Frederik Hogenboom, Flavius Frasincar, Kim Schouten, and Otto van der Meer. 2013. Semantics-based information extraction for detecting economic events. *Multimedia Tools and Applications*, 64(1):27–52.

Nancy C. Ide and Keith Suderman. 2004. The American National Corpus First Release. In *LREC 2004 — Proceedings of the 4th International Conference on Language Resources and Evaluation. In Memory of Antonio Zampolli. Lisbon, Portugal, 24-30 May, 2004*, pages 1681–1684.

Kazushi Ikeda, Gen Hattori, Chihiro Ono, Hideki Asoh, and Teruo Higashino. 2013. Twitter user profiling based on text and community mining for market analysis. *Knowledge-Based Systems*, 51:35–47.

Takakazu Imada, Yusuke Inoue, Lei Chen, Syunya Doi, Tian Nie, Chen Zhao, Takehito Utsuro, and Yasuhide Kawada. 2016. Analyzing time series changes of correlation between market share and concerns on companies measured through search engine suggests. In *LREC 2016 — Proceedings of the 10th International Conference on Language Resources and Evaluation. Portorož, Slovenia, 23-28 May 2016*, pages 1917–1923.

Min Jiang, Yang Huang, Jung-Wei Fan, Buzhou Tang, Joshua C. Denny, and Hua Xu. 2015. Parsing clinical text: How good are the state-of-the-art parsers? *BMC Medical Informatics and Decision Making*, 15(Suppl 1):S2.

Siavash Kazemian, Shunan Zhao, and Gerald Penn. 2014. Evaluating sentiment analysis evaluation: A case study in securities trading. In *WASSA 2014 — Proceedings of the 5th Workshop on Computational Approaches to Subjectivity, Sentiment and Social Media Analysis @ ACL 2014. Baltimore, Maryland, USA, June 27, 2014*, pages 119–127.

Wiltrud Kessler, Roman Klinger, and Jonas Kuhn. 2015. Towards opinion mining from reviews for the prediction of product rankings. In *WASSA 2015 — Proceedings of the 6th Workshop on Computational Approaches to Subjectivity, Sentiment and Social Media Analysis @ EMNLP 2015. Lisbon, Portugal, 17 September 2015*, pages 51–57.

Wiltrud Kessler and Jonas Kuhn. 2013. Detection of product comparisons: How far does an out-of-the-box semantic role labeling system take you? In *EMNLP 2013 — Proceedings of the 2013 Conference on Empirical Methods in Natural Language Processing. Seattle, Washington, USA, 18-21 October 2013*, pages 1892–1897.

Wiltrud Kessler and Jonas Kuhn. 2014. A corpus of comparisons in product reviews. In *LREC 2014 — Proceedings of the 9th International Conference on Language Resources and Evaluation. Reykjavik, Iceland, May 26-31, 2014*, pages 2242–2248.

Brayden G. King. 2015. Organizational actors, character, and Selznicks theory of organizations. In Matthew S. Kraatz, editor, *Institutions and Ideals: Philip Selznicks Legacy for Organizational Studies*, pages 149–174. Emerald Group.

Brayden G. King, Teppo Felin, and David A. Whetten. 2010. Finding the organization in organizational theory. A meta-theory of the organization as a social actor. *Organization Science*, 21(1):290–305.

Antonina Kloptchenko, Tomas Eklund, Barbro Back, Jonas Karlsson, Hannu Vanharanta, and Ari Visa. 2004. Combining data and text mining techniques for analysing financial reports. *Intelligent Systems in Accounting, Finance and Management*, 12(1):29–41.

Shimon Kogan, Dimitry Levin, Bryan R. Routledge, Jacob S. Sagi, and Noah A. Smith. 2009. Predicting risk from financial reports with regression. In *NAACL-HLT 2009 — Human Language Technologies: Proceedings of the 2009 Annual Conference of the North American Chapter of the Association for Computational Linguistics. Boulder, Colorado, USA, May 31 - June 5, 2009*, volume 1, pages 272–280.

B. Shravan Kumar and Vadlamani Ravi. 2016. A survey of the applications of text mining in financial domain. *Knowledge-Based Systems*, 114:128–147.

Marc Kupietz and Harald Lüngen. 2014. Recent developments in DeReKo. In *LREC 2014 — Proceedings of the 9th International Conference on Language Resources and Evaluation. Reykjavik, Iceland, May 26-31, 2014*, pages 2378–2385.

Veronika Laippala, Timo Viljanen, Antti Airola, Jenna Kanerva, Sanna Salanterä, Tapio Salakoski, and Filip Ginter. 2014. Statistical parsing of varieties of clinical Finnish. *Artificial Intelligence in Medicine*, 61(3):131–136.

Heeyoung Lee, Mihai Surdeanu, Bill MacCartney, and Daniel Jurafsky. 2014. On the importance of text analysis for stock price prediction. In *LREC 2014 — Proceedings of the 9th International Conference on Language Resources and Evaluation. Reykjavik, Iceland, May 26-31, 2014*, pages 1170–1175.

Els Lefever and Véronique Hoste. 2016. A classification-based approach to economic event detection in Dutch news text. In *LREC 2016 — Proceedings of the 10th International Conference on Language Resources and Evaluation. Portorož, Slovenia, 23-28 May 2016*, pages 330–335.

Qing Li, Yan Chen, Jun Wang, Yuanzhu Chen, and Hsinchun Chen. 2018. Web media and stock markets : A survey and future directions from a big data perspective. *IEEE Transactions on Knowledge and Data Engineering*, 30(2):381–399.

Qing Li, TieJun Wang, Ping Li, Ling Liu, Qixu Gong, and Yuanzhu Chen. 2014. The effect of news and public mood on stock movements. *Information Sciences*, 278:826–840.

Kung-Yee Liang and Scott L Zeger. 1986. Longitudinal data analysis using generalized linear models. *Biometrika*, 73(1):13–22.

Bing Liu. 2015. *Sentiment Analysis: Mining Opinions, Sentiments, and Emotions*. Cambridge University Press, New York, NY.

Ling Liu, Jing Wu, Ping Li, and Qing Li. 2015. A social-media-based approach to predicting stock comovement. *Expert Systems with Applications*, 42(8):3893–3901.

Tim Loughran and Bill McDonald. 2011. When is a liability not a liability? Textual analysis, dictionaries, and 10-Ks. *Journal of Finance*, 66(1):35–65.

Hsin Min Lu, Hsinchun Chen, Tsai Jyh Chen, Mao Wei Hung, and Shu Hsing Li. 2010. Financial text mining: Supporting decision making using Web 2.0 content. *IEEE Intelligent Systems*, 25(2):78–82.

Ronny Luss and Alexandre d'Aspremont. 2015. Predicting abnormal returns from news using text classification. *Quantitative Finance*, 15(6):999–1012.

Pekka Malo, Ankur Sinha, Pekka Korhonen, Jyrki Wallenius, and Pyry Takala. 2014. Good debt or bad debt: Detecting semantic orientations in economic texts. *Journal of the Association for Information Science and Technology*, 65(4):782–796.

Mitchell P. Marcus, Beatrice Santorini, and Mary Ann Marcinkiewicz. 1993. Building a large annotated corpus of English: The Penn Treebank. *Computational Linguistics*, 19(2):313–330.

Renate E Meyer and Markus A Höllerer. 2010. Meaning structures in a contested issue field: A topographic map of shareholder value in Austria. *Academy of Management Journal*, 53(6):1241–1262.

Andrew Moore, Paul Rayson, and Steven Young. 2016. Domain adaptation using stock market prices to refine sentiment dictionaries. In *ESA 2016 — Proceedings of the [6th] Workshop on Emotion and Sentiment Analysis @ LREC 2016. Portorož, Slovenia, 23 May 2016*, pages 63–66.

Arjun Mukherjee, Bing Liu, and Natalie Glance. 2012. Spotting fake reviewer groups in consumer reviews. In *WWW '12 — Proceedings of the 21st Annual Conference on World Wide Web. Lyon, France, April 16-20, 2012*, pages 191–200.

Arman Khadjeh Nassirtoussi, Saeed Aghabozorgi, Teh-Ying Wah, and David Chek Ling Ngo. 2014. Text mining for market prediction: A systematic review. *Expert Systems with Applications*, 41(16):7653–7670.

Dean Neu, Hussein Warsame, and Kathryn Pedwell. 1998. Managing public impressions: Environmental disclosures in annual reports. *Accounting, Organizations and Society*, 23(3):265–282.

Thien Hai Nguyen and Kiyoaki Shirai. 2015. Topic modeling based sentiment analysis on social media for stock market prediction. In *ACL-IJCNLP 2015 — Proceedings of the 53rd Annual Meeting of the Association for Computational Linguistics & 7th International Joint Conference on Natural Language Processing of the Asian Federation of Natural Language Processing. Beijing, China, July 26-31, 2015*, pages 1354–1364.

Nuno Oliveira, Paulo Cortez, and Nelson Areal. 2016. Stock market sentiment lexicon acquisition using microblogging data and statistical measures. *Decision Support Systems*, 85:62–73.

Martha Palmer, Daniel Gildea, and Paul Kingsbury. 2005. The Proposition Bank: An annotated corpus of semantic roles. *Computational Linguistics*, 31(1):71–106.

Viktor Pekar and Jane Binner. 2017. Forecasting consumer spending from purchase intentions expressed on social media. In *WASSA 2017 — Proceedings of the 8th Workshop on Computational Approaches to Subjectivity, Sentiment and Social Media Analysis @ EMNLP 2017. Copenhagen, Denmark, September 8, 2017*, pages 92–101.

Reid Pryzant, Young-joo Chung, and Daniel Jurafsky. 2017. Predicting sales from the language of product descriptions. In *SIGIR eCom 2017 — Proceedings of the ACM SIGIR Workshop on eCommerce. Tokyo, Japan, August 11, 2017*.

Xin Ying Qiu and Padmini Srinivasan. 2014. Supervised learning models to predict firm performance with annual reports: An empirical study. *Journal of the Association for Information Science and Technology*, 65(2):400–413.

Michael Rechenthin, W. Nick Street, and Padmini Srinivasan. 2013. Stock chatter: Using stock sentiment to predict price direction. *Algorithmic Finance*, 2(3-4):169–196.

Navid Rekabsaz, Mihai Lupu, Artem Baklanov, Allan Hanbury, Alexander Dür, and Linda Anderson. 2017. Volatility prediction using financial disclosures sentiments with word embedding-based ir

models. In *ACL 2017 — Proceedings of the 55th Annual Meeting of the Association for Computational Linguistics. Vancouver, British Columbia, Canada, July 30 - August 4, 2017*, volume 1: Long Papers, pages 1712–1721.

Brian A Rutherford. 2005. Genre analysis of corporate annual report narratives: A corpus linguistics-based approach. *The Journal of Business Communication*, 42(4):349–378.

Shigeyuki Sakaki, Francine Chen, Mandy Korpusik, and Yan-Ying Chen. 2016. Corpus for customer purchase behavior prediction in social media. In *LREC 2016 — Proceedings of the 10th International Conference on Language Resources and Evaluation. Portorož, Slovenia, 23-28 May 2016*, pages 2976–2980.

Saskia Schön, Veselina Mironova, Aleksandra Gabryszak, and Leonhard Hennig. 2018. A corpus study and annotation schema for named entity recognition and relation extraction of business products. In *LREC 2018 — Proceedings of the 11th International Conference on Language Resources and Evaluation. Miyazaki, Japan, May 7-12, 2018*, pages 4445–4451.

Robert P. Schumaker and Hsinchun Chen. 2009. Textual analysis of stock market prediction using breaking financial news: The AZFINTEXT system. *ACM Transactions on Information Systems*, 27(2):#12.

Jianfeng Si, Arjun Mukherjee, Bing Liu, Sinno Jialin Pan, Qing Li, and Huayi Li. 2014. Exploiting social relations and sentiment for stock prediction. In *EMNLP 2014 — Proceedings of the 2014 Conference on Empirical Methods in Natural Language Processing. Doha, Qatar, October 25-29, 2014*, pages 1139–1145.

Herbert A. Simon. 1991. Organizations and markets. *Journal of Economic Perspectives*, 5(2):25–44.

Anna Stavrianou and Caroline Brun. 2015. Expert recommendations based on opinion mining of user-generated product reviews. *Computational Intelligence*, 31(1):165–183.

Pyry Takala, Pekka Malo, Ankur Sinha, and Oskar Ahlgren. 2014. Gold-standard for topic-specific sentiment analysis of economic texts. In *LREC 2014 — Proceedings of the 9th International Conference on Language Resources and Evaluation. Reykjavik, Iceland, May 26-31, 2014*, pages 2152–2157.

Yi-jie Tang and Hsin-Hsi Chen. 2014. FADR: A system for recognizing false online advertisements. In *ACL 2014 — Proceedings of the 52nd Annual Meeting of the Association for Computational Linguistics: System Demonstrations. Baltimore, Maryland, USA, June 23-24, 2014*, pages 103–108.

Fangbo Tao, Bo Zhao, Ariel Fuxman, Yang Li, and Jiawei Han. 2015. Leveraging pattern semantics for extracting entities in enterprises. In *WWW 2015 —*

Proceedings of the 24th International Conference on World Wide Web. Florence, Italy, May 18–22, 2015, pages 1078–1088.

Katrin Tomanek, Joachim Wermter, and Udo Hahn. 2007. A reappraisal of sentence and token splitting for life sciences documents. In *MedInfo 2007 — Proceedings of the 12th World Congress on Health (Medical) Informatics. Building Sustainable Health Systems. Brisbane, Australia, August 20-24, 2007*, number 129 in Studies in Health Technology and Informatics, pages 524–528, Amsterdam. IOS Press.

Andrew Trotman, Jon Degenhardt, and Surya Kallumadi. 2017. The architecture of EBAY SEARCH. In *SIGIR eCom 2017 — Proceedings of the ACM SIGIR Workshop on eCommerce. Tokyo, Japan, August 11, 2017*.

Ming-Feng Tsai and Chuan-Ju Wang. 2017. On the risk prediction and analysis of soft information in finance reports. *European Journal of Operational Research*, 257(1):243–250.

Takaaki Tsunoda, Takashi Inui, and Satoshi Sekine. 2015. Utilizing review analysis to suggest product advertisement improvements. In *WASSA 2015 — Proceedings of the 6th Workshop on Computational Approaches to Subjectivity, Sentiment and Social Media Analysis @ EMNLP 2015. Lisbon, Portugal, 17 September 2015*, pages 41–50.

Marjan Van De Kauter, Diane Breesch, and Véronique Hoste. 2015. Fine-grained analysis of explicit and implicit sentiment in financial news articles. *Expert Systems with Applications*, 42(11):4999–5010.

Damir Vandic, Steven S. Aanen, Flavius Frasincar, and Uzay Kaymak. 2017. Dynamic facet ordering for faceted product search engines. *IEEE Transactions on Knowledge and Data Engineering*, 29(5):1004–1016.

Martin Žnidaršič, Jasmina Smailović, Jan Gorše, Miha Grčar, Igor Mozetič, and Senja Pollak. 2018. Trust and doubt terms in financial tweets and periodic reports. In *FNP 2018 — Proceedings of the 1st Financial Narrative Processing Workshop @ LREC 2018. Miyazaki, Japan, 7 May 2018*, pages 59–65.

Hao Wang and Martin Ester. 2014. A sentiment-aligned topic model for product aspect rating prediction. In *EMNLP 2014 — Proceedings of the 2014 Conference on Empirical Methods in Natural Language Processing. Doha, Qatar, October 25-29, 2014*, pages 1192–1202.

William Yang Wang and Zhenhao Hua. 2014. A semi-parametric Gaussian copula regression model for predicting financial risks from earnings calls. In *ACL 2014 — Proceedings of the 52nd Annual Meeting of the Association for Computational Linguistics. Baltimore, Maryland, USA, June 22-27, 2014*, pages 1155–1165.

Albert Weichselbraun, Daniel Streiff, and Arno Scharl. 2015. Consolidating heterogeneous enterprise data for named entity linking and Web intelligence. *International Journal on Artificial Intelligence Tools*, 24(2):#1540008.

Boyi Xie, Rebecca J. Passonneau, Leon Wu, and Germán G. Creamer. 2013. Semantic frames to predict stock price movement. In *ACL 2013 — Proceedings of the 51st Annual Meeting of the Association for Computational Linguistics. Sofia, Bulgaria, August 4-9, 2013*, pages 873–883.

Frank Z. Xing, Erik Cambria, and Roy E. Welsch. 2018. Natural language based financial forecasting: A survey. *Artificial Intelligence Review*, 50(1):49–73.

Chao Yang, Shimei Pan, Jalal U. Mahmud, Huahai Yang, and Padmini Srinivasan. 2015. Using personal traits for brand preference prediction. In *EMNLP 2015 — Proceedings of the 2015 Conference on Empirical Methods in Natural Language Processing. Lisbon, Portugal, 17-21 September 2015*, pages 86–96.

Kristi Yuthas, Rodney Rogers, and Jesse F Dillard. 2002. Communicative action and corporate annual reports. *Journal of Business Ethics*, 41(1-2):141–157.

Yongzheng Zhang and Marco Pennacchiotti. 2013. Predicting purchase behaviors from social media. In *WWW '13 — Proceedings of the 22nd International Conference on World Wide Web. Rio de Janeiro, Brazil, May 13-17, 2013*, pages 1521–1532.

A   Supplemental Material

In general, the estimating technique must address the main characteristics of the data at hand. Due to the repeated observations over the eight years (from 2008 to 2015), the investigated cases are not independent from each other which increases the likelihood of autocorrelation in the data. In order to appropriately deal with this issue, we employ the generalized estimating equations (GEE) method (Liang and Zeger, 1986). We report population-average estimators with fixed effects that allow us to control for organizational differences we cannot account for directly. Also, this model allows for omitting observable but stable organizational characteristics. We use a normal distribution for modeling the dependent variable.

	ROE	Valence	Arousal	Dom.	lnEmpls	lnAssets	Sales/Empl.	Sales/Assets	Country
ROE	1								
Valence	.03	1							
Arousal	-.02	-.68	1						
Dominance	.56	.90	-.70	1					
ln(Employees)	.10	-.05	.22	-.12	1				
ln(Assets)	.50	.02	-.19	-.10	.77	1			
Sales/Employee	-.02	.06	-.06	.22	-.29	.07	1		
Sales/Assets	.01	.00	-.03	.54	-.97	-.37	-.06	1	
Country	-.58	-.12	.07	-.37	.13	.83	.08	.50	1

Table 3: Correlation matrix of independent, dependent and control variables in the GEE model. 'Country' is coded as Germany(GER)= 1, UK= 0.

	Model I: Controls			Model II: Explanatory			Model III: Full		
	Beta	S.E.	Sig.	Beta	S.E.	Sig.	Beta	S.E.	Sig.
Arousal				-.067	.055	.228	-.158	.040	.000
Dominance				-.019	.040	.636	.016	.061	.795
Arousal*Country							.189	.047	.000
Dominance*Country							.022	.066	.737
lnEmployees	.080	.030	.007	.085	.312	.007	.082	.031	.008
lnAssets	-.058	.030	.050	-.057	.030	.056	-.056	.030	.059
Sales/Employee	.049	.023	.037	.048	.024	.041	.050	.024	.035
Sales/Assets	.004	.038	.915	.004	.038	.914	-.004	.038	.915
Country	-.191	.088	.030	-.196	.098	.046	-.159	.098	.103
Constant	.253	.357	.480	.196	.366	.591	.191	.368	.603

Table 4: Results of GEE panel regression with dependent variable ROE lagged by one year and interaction effects of arousal and dominance with the country dummy (GER=1). Columns give the respective slope coefficient (Beta), standard error (S.E.) and p-value (Sig.). The three models differ in the set of variables taken into account. The number of cases is 1,127 for each model (one AR per corporation per year in the application's subsample of the corpus).

Word Embeddings-Based Uncertainty Detection in Financial Disclosures

Christoph Kilian Theil, **Sanja Štajner** and **Heiner Stuckenschmidt**
Data and Web Science Group
University of Mannheim, Germany
{christoph, sanja, heiner}@informatik.uni-mannheim.de

Abstract

In this paper, we use NLP techniques to detect linguistic uncertainty in financial disclosures. Leveraging general-domain and domain-specific word embedding models, we automatically expand an existing dictionary of uncertainty triggers. We furthermore examine how an expert filtering affects the quality of such an expansion. We show that the dictionary expansions significantly improve regressions on stock return volatility. Lastly, we prove that the expansions significantly boost the automatic detection of uncertain sentences.

1 Introduction

Despite its real world impact in tasks like volatility prediction, the automatic detection of linguistic uncertainty has been left relatively untouched in finance. Motivated by this research gap, we created the first classifier capable of detecting uncertain sentences in so-called *10-Ks*. These annual reports are required by the U.S. Securities and Exchange Commission (SEC) and give a comprehensive overview of a company's business activities. We selected this disclosure type since it has to be filed by all public companies in the U.S., thus ensuring a large sample size. Furthermore, it is the only disclosure type for which a tailored dictionary resource exists.

1.1 Loughran & McDonald's Dictionary

As basis for our experiments, we took an existing financial domain dictionary containing 297 uncertain terms. This dictionary has been shown to possess explanatory power of future stock return volatility (Loughran and McDonald, 2011) and is the only of its kind specifically designed for

10-Ks. Its creators developed it "with emphasis on the general notion of imprecision rather than exclusively focusing on risk" (Loughran and Mc-Donald, 2011, p. 45). As this quote indicates, on one hand, the dictionary contains terms marking imprecision (e.g. "could", "may", "probably", "somewhat"). On the other hand, it contains terms referring to real-worldly risk and uncertainty (e.g. "anomaly", "risk", "uncertainty", "volatility").

1.2 Contributions

We automatically expanded Loughran and Mc-Donald's (2011) uncertainty dictionary by adding semantically close candidate terms according to word embeddings. Apart from training our own domain-specific embedding model, we compared such an expansion to one using a general-domain embedding model. Moreover, we investigated whether manual filtering of candidate terms by a domain expert can further improve the results. We evaluated the quality of our expansions in both a set of regressions on stock return volatility and a binary sentence classification task by posing two research questions:

- **RQ1** How do a general-domain and a domain-specific expansion compare?

- **RQ2** How do an automatic and a semi-automatic, expert-filtered expansion compare?

We show that our unfiltered domain-specific expansion significantly increases the explanatory power of regressions on stock return volatility over the plain dictionary. We furthermore introduce a dataset of annual reports newly annotated for this study and train a binary classifier distinguishing uncertain from certain sentences. Again, the domain-specific expansion significantly improves the classification performance over the plain dictionary. In this case, however, the expert-filtering

Proceedings of the First Workshop on Economics and Natural Language Processing, pages 32–37
Melbourne, Australia, July 20, 2018. ©2018 Association for Computational Linguistics

provides a small performance increase over the fully automatic expansion.

2 Related Work

Loughran and McDonald (2011) introduced financial dictionaries spanning the categories of *positive, negative, litigious, strong modal, weak modal*, and—most important for us—*uncertain* words. Perhaps not surprisingly, they find that the cumulative tf–idf of *uncertain* terms in a set of 10-Ks shares a positive and highly significant relation with future stock return volatility. To quantify the improvement of our new expansions over this dictionary, we use a regression setup similar to their subsequent paper (Loughran and McDonald, 2014).

Tsai and Wang (2014) automatically expanded said dictionaries by training word embeddings and adding the 20 most cosine similar terms to each original dictionary term. Using a dataset of 10-Ks, they show that this expansion improves a prediction of future stock return volatility. In contrast to them, we provide a systematic analysis how a domain-specific vs. a general-domain (RQ1) and an automatic vs. a semi-automatic expansion (RQ2) perform in a set of regressions. Furthermore, for the first time in the community, we perform a binary sentence classification task on 10-Ks to assess directly whether our models are indeed suitable to detect linguistic uncertainty.

Theil et al. (2017) created the first classifier capable to detect uncertain sentences in the financial domain. Yet, they sample their sentences from earnings call transcripts, a largely different disclosure type than 10-Ks. Apart from typical characteristics of spoken language such as less structure and more spontaneity, these disclosures are voluntary and thus usually less available. As previous studies have hinted that analyzing the language of 10-Ks can help to explain uncertainty of the information environment (Loughran and McDonald, 2011, 2014), we were further motivated to create the first sentence classifier for 10-Ks.

3 Data

We downloaded Loughran and McDonald's (2011) dictionary[1] of 297 financial uncertainty triggers such as "may", "probably", or "volatility". From now on, we refer to this dictionary as *Unc*. We further downloaded all

---

[1] https://sraf.nd.edu/textual-analysis/resources

220,565 10-Ks during 1994 to 2015 from the SEC's database EDGAR[2]. We removed duplicates and filings shorter than 250 words, thus leaving 203,321 files. We divided this set into three non-overlapping subsets: First, using word2vec (Mikolov et al., 2013) with standard parameters, we deployed 124,830 10-Ks (approximately 2.3 billion words) to train a domain-specific embedding model. As benchmark, we also retrieved Google's generic word2vec embedding model,[3] which was trained on approximately 100 billion words from the Google News dataset.

Second, we used 76,991 10-Ks in our regressions. For each instance, we retrieved stock pricing data from the databases CRSP[4] and CRSP/Compustat Merged. To facilitate replication, our data screening and parsing procedures are described in greater detail in our Online Appendix.[5] It further contains all textual and financial data needed to replicate our regressions.

Third, we used a random sample of 1,500 10-Ks for the classification task. Out of these, we randomly sampled 100 sentences and let two annotators of financial and linguistic knowledge co-annotate them as either *certain* or *uncertain*. The guidelines which we gave to our annotators can be found in the Online Appendix.

It has to be noted that the task of evaluating uncertainty as an inherently subjective semantic concept—especially in such a specialized domain as finance—is of particular intricacy. First, consider the following sentence, which both annotators labeled *uncertain*:

Example 3.1. "These factors raise substantial doubt regarding the Company's ability to continue as a going concern."

In contrast, consider the following sentence, on which the annotators disagreed; words and phrases considered to be uncertainty triggers by the annotator proposing an *uncertain* label are underlined:

Example 3.2. "Fidelity is subject to <u>interest rate risk</u> to the degree that its interest-bearing liabilities, <u>primarily deposits</u> with short and medium term maturities, <u>mature or reprice at different rates</u> than its interest-earning assets."

This sentence references "risk" and contains

---

[2] https://www.sec.gov/edgar.shtml
[3] https://code.google.com/archive/p/word2vec
[4] http://www.crsp.com
[5] http://dws.informatik.uni-mannheim.de/en/people/researchers/christoph-kilian-theil/

additional imprecisions, which speaks in favor of an *uncertain* label. Yet, the referenced risk is nonopaque and said imprecisions could be attributed to legal requirements as inherent to any regulated corporate disclosure; hence, a case could also be made for an *certain* label.

Nevertheless, the IAA measured as κ (Cohen, 1960) was 0.73, which can be considered "substantial" (Landis and Koch, 1977). Notably, Ganter and Strube (2009) report an even lower pairwise IAA with $0.45 \leq \kappa \leq 0.80, \bar{x}_\kappa = 0.56$ for an annotation of Wikipedia sentences as *certain* or *uncertain*. Despite making use of highly trained domain experts, Štajner et al. (2017) also obtained a lower IAA with $0.47 \leq \kappa \leq 0.70, \bar{x}_\kappa = 0.61$ for a comparable annotation task. They sampled their sentences from transcribed debates held by the U.S. central bank's monetary policy committee (FOMC).

Given our comparably high IAA, we were confident of our annotation quality and let the first annotator annotate an additional 900 sentences, thus forming our newly created dataset REPORTS. Out of its 1,000 sentences, 870 were labeled *certain* and 130 were labeled *uncertain*. This new dataset can also be found in our Online Appendix as useful resource for others to advance the field.

4 Methodology

4.1 Expanding the Dictionary

To answer RQ1, we first determined the 20 most cosine similar terms according to the generic embedding model for each of the 297 terms of *Unc*. We chose 20 as the number of added terms since this is the value suggested by Tsai and Wang (2014). After lowercasing, we removed 28 anomalous tokens (e.g. "##.million"), 1,657 *n*-grams, and 2,139 duplicates. We excluded *n*-grams, since *Unc* contains only unigrams and we wanted to keep its expansions comparable. We added the remaining 2,036 terms to *Unc* and thus created *UncGen* with 2,333 terms.

For our domain-specific model, we derived a list of 5,820 candidate terms and removed 1,947 duplicates. We did not lowercase in this case, as this was already part of our preprocessing. We again added the remaining 3,873 terms to *Unc* and thus created *UncSpec* with 4,170 terms. Remarkably, *UncGen* and *UncSpec* share an overlap of 458 (23% and 12%) of the newly added terms, which indicates that they employ a largely differ-

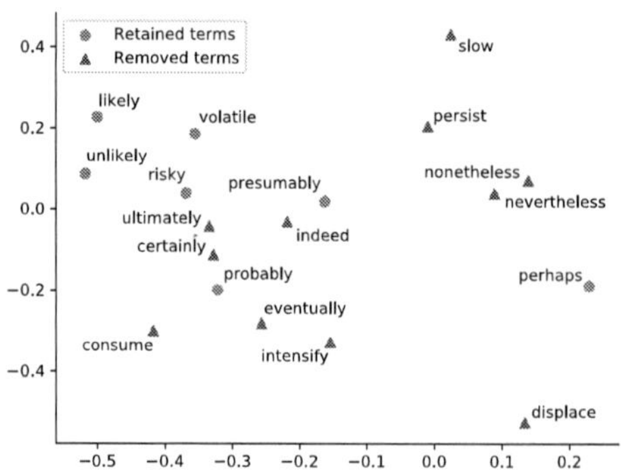

Figure 1: Candidate terms for "probably" in our domain-specific embedding model. Terms retained/removed by the annotator are marked by dots/triangles. Dimensionality is reduced through t-SNE (van der Maaten and Hinton, 2008).

ent vocabulary. An exemplary overview of added terms according to both models can be found in our Online Appendix.

We found that antonyms—despite their opposite meaning—were frequently embedded in similar semantic spaces. Coalescing relations of synonymy and antonymy is a well-known and often undesired property of distributional models (Mohammed et al., 2008). Hence, it can be explained why both *UncGen* as well as *UncSpec* contain the token "certainly" as cosine similar term to "probably" (similarity of 0.68 and 0.45, respectively). In addition, other irrelevant terms (e.g. "event", "significance") appeared frequently in close proximity to uncertain terms.

This motivated us to explore how manual filtering could improve the expanded dictionaries (RQ2). Therefore, we let an annotator of both financial and linguistic domain knowledge evaluate and remove such terms he deemed inappropriate to cover uncertainty. Figure 1 provides an exemplary visualization of this procedure. Thus, we created the dictionaries *UncGen*$_{exp}$ with 538 and *UncSpec*$_{exp}$ with 475 terms. Notably, the filtering caused the vocabulary of both lists to converge, as they now shared an overlap of 241 (45% and 51%) of the added terms. Finally, we created the combinations *UncGen+UncSpec* and *UncGen*$_{exp}$+*UncSpec*$_{exp}$. An overview of all dictionaries can be found in Table 1.

Table 1: Number of uncertainty triggers per dictionary.

Dictionary	# of Triggers
Unc	297
Automatic Expansions:	
UncGen	2,333
UncSpec	4,170
UncGen+UncSpec	5,748
Expert-Aided Expansions:	
UncGen$_{exp}$	538
UncSpec$_{exp}$	475
UncGen$_{exp}$+UncSpec$_{exp}$	652

Table 2: Results of the regression on volatility. Standard errors are clustered by year and industry. Coefficients are standardized with a mean of zero and a standard deviation of one.

Dictionary	Coefficient	t	R^2
Unc	0.016*	2.28	47.91%
UncGen	0.014*	2.20	47.90%
UncGen$_{exp}$	0.017*	2.56	47.91%
UncSpec	0.034***	3.90	47.96%
UncSpec$_{exp}$	0.020*	2.68	47.91%
UncGen+UncSpec	0.032***	3.67	47.95%
UncGen$_{exp}$+UncSpec$_{exp}$	0.017*	2.59	47.91%

$^*p \leq 0.05$, $^{**}p \leq 0.01$, $^{***}p \leq 0.001$

4.2 Regressing Uncertainty on Volatility

To assess the real world impact of our problem, we performed event studies measuring the association of linguistic uncertainty in our set of 76,991 10-Ks with *volatility*, a common measure of financial uncertainty. To be comparable with previous work (Loughran and McDonald, 2011, 2014), we measure volatility as the deviation between the expected and the actual returns after the report's filing date in terms of root mean square error (RMSE). We calculate the expected returns estimating market models (Sharpe, 1963) using trading days $[6, 28]$ relative to the filing date.

In addition, following Loughran and McDonald (2014), we used an extensive set of control variables: the intercepts α and the RMSE from market models using trading days $[-252, -6]$ as indicators of *historic performance* and *historic volatility*. The *filing period abnormal return* as absolute value of the buy-and-hold return in trading days $[0, 1]$ minus the buy-and-hold return of the market index. The *firm size* as current stock price multiplied by the number of outstanding shares. The *book-to-market* ratio, a valuation measure, calculated as the book value of equity divided by the market value of equity. Here, we only considered firms with a positive book value and winsorized at the 1% level. Lastly, we used a *NASDAQ dummy* variable set to one if the firm is listed on the NASDAQ at the time of the 10-K filing, otherwise zero.

We calculated the cumulative tf–idf of all uncertain terms according to the dictionary *Unc* and its six expansions (see Table 1). Then, we conducted seven regressions with each containing uncertainty gauged via the respective dictionary as main independent variable, the control variables, and postfiling volatility as dependent variable. This setup allows us to quantify financial uncertainty likely induced by the filing event. All regressions include an intercept, calendar year dummies, and Fama and French (1997) 48-industry dummies for time- and industry-fixed effects. For brevity, we only report the key statistics for our main independent variables—a more detailed overview with all control variables can be found in our Online Appendix.

4.3 Creating a Classifier of Uncertainty

We used the seven dictionaries (Table 1) as feature sets in the binary classification task. As feature representation, we tried both relative term frequency (tf) as well as term frequency–inverse document frequency (tf–idf). Next, using Weka Experimenter (Hall et al., 2009), we applied six machine algorithms in a 10-fold cross-validation setup with ten repetitions: Logistic Regression (le Cessie and van Houwelingen, 1992); SMO, the Weka implementation of Support Vector Machine (Platt, 1999); JRip, the Weka implementation of RIPPER (Cohen, 1995); J48, the Weka implementation of C4.5 decision tree (Quinlan, 1993); Random Forest (Breiman, 2001); and a Convolutional Neural Network (Amtén, 2014). As a JRip classifier outperformed the other five, we only report its performance—for the same reason, we only report the results for tf–idf weighting. The full results according to all algorithms and both feature representations can be found in our Online Appendix.

5 Results and Discussion

5.1 Regression

The results of our regressions are depicted in Table 2. In all regressions, uncertainty and postfiling volatility have a positive statistical relation. This relation is significant ($p \leq 0.05$) for

Table 3: Results of the classification task for the *uncertain* class of REPORTS. The best results are boldfaced and significant performance increases ($\alpha = 0.05$) over *Unc* are marked with asterisks.

Dictionary	P	R	F	A
Unc	0.65	0.49	0.54	89.66%
UncGen	0.66	0.51	0.56	89.86%
UncGen$_{exp}$	0.67	0.52	0.56	90.05%
UncSpec	**0.69***	0.54*	0.58*	90.31%
UncSpec$_{exp}$	0.67	**0.56***	**0.59***	**90.37%**
UncGen+UncSpec	**0.69***	0.52	0.57	90.30%
UncGen$_{exp}$+UncSpec$_{exp}$	0.66	0.54	0.58	90.07%
Majority Class (certain)	0.00	0.00	0.00	87.00%

Unc, *UncGen*, *UncGen$_{exp}$*, *UncSpec$_{exp}$*, as well as *UncGen$_{exp}$+UncSpec$_{exp}$*, and highly significant ($p \leq 0.001$) for *UncSpec* and *UncGen+UncSpec*.

The strength of this association is also the highest for both *UncSpec* and *UncGen+UncSpec* (0.034 and 0.032), twice as high than that of *Unc* (0.016). This shows that these expansions have a decisively higher explanatory power of volatility. Furthermore, concerning RQ1, the regressions seem to benefit most from a specific instead of a generic dictionary expansion. Additionally, with regard to RQ2, the expert filtering does not improve the results—in some cases, it even worsens them. As shown in Table 1, our expert annotator retained a relatively small subset of the candidate terms (23% of *UncGen* and 11% of *UncSpec*). Such a rigid filtering causes a smaller coverage of the expansions and furthermore carries the danger of false negative errors. We hypothesize that the effect of erroneously added terms is already mitigated through tf–idf weighting, thus rendering manual work unnecessary.

Above discussed coefficients might appear small, as a one standard deviation increase of *Unc-Spec* explains only a 3.4% of such an increase in volatility. However, this is in line with previous research attesting that the "economic magnitude of the soft information is somewhat limited" (Loughran and McDonald, 2016, p. 1202).

5.2 Classification

Table 3 shows the results of the classification task on the newly created dataset REPORTS. Performance is evaluated in terms of precision (P), recall (R), F_1 score (F) on the *uncertain* class, and in terms of overall accuracy (A). Additionally, significant performance increases over *Unc* were determined through paired t-tests with $\alpha = 0.05$.

The highest precision (0.69) is obtained through *UncSpec* and *UncGen+UncSpec*, which significantly outperform *Unc*. *UncSpec$_{exp}$* scores highest in terms of recall (0.56), which again is significantly higher than that of *Unc*. This value in combination with a relatively high precision (0.67) makes the former feature set the strongest overall in terms of an F_1 score of 0.59, thus significantly exceeding *Unc* and *UncGen$_{exp}$*.

Overall, the high precision of *UncSpec* and *UncGen+UncSpec* coincides with the regressions (see Section 5.1), where both already yielded the highest coefficients. Another similarity are the implications for our research questions: Again, the domain-specific expansion performs best (RQ1), while the expert filtering does not provide visible improvements (RQ2).

Out of the newly added terms of *UncGen$_{exp}$*, 24 are contained in the 130 sentences labeled as *uncertain*. This stands in contrast to 29 matches with the terms of *UncSpec$_{exp}$*, which again indicates an advantage of the domain-specific model. The domain-dependent and legalese language of the latter reflects in matching terms such as "uninsured", "more-likely-than-not", and "interpretive".

In summary, our results show that for the given task, training own domain-specific word embedding models gives an advantage over relying on generic, off-the-shelf solutions. Lastly, the results reveal that the manual filtering of candidate terms has only a negligible impact on performance.

6   Conclusion

In this paper, we expanded a dictionary of financial uncertainty triggers through both a generic and a domain-specific embedding model. In a set of financial regressions, we showed that our domain-specific expansion shares a two times greater and highly significant association with subsequent volatility than the plain dictionary. Furthermore, we presented a newly annotated dataset of annual reports and showed that the dictionary expansions significantly boost the performance in a binary classification task of uncertain sentences.

Acknowledgments

This work was supported by the SFB 884 on the Political Economy of Reforms at the University of Mannheim (project C4), funded by the German Research Foundation (DFG).

References

Johannes Amtén. 2014. Neural network plugin for Weka. https://github.com/amten/NeuralNetwork. Accessed on January 16, 2018.

Leo Breiman. 2001. Random forests. *Machine Learning*, 45(1):5–32.

Saskia le Cessie and Hans C. van Houwelingen. 1992. Ridge estimators in logistic regression. *Applied Statistics*, 41(1):191–201.

Jacob Cohen. 1960. A coefficient of agreement for nominal scales. *Educational and Psychological Measurement*, 20(1):41–48.

William W. Cohen. 1995. Fast effective rule induction. In *Proceedings of the ICML*, pages 115–123.

Eugene F. Fama and Kenneth R. French. 1997. Industry costs of equity. *Journal of Financial Economics*, 43:153–193.

Viola Ganter and Michael Strube. 2009. Finding hedges by chasing weasels: Hedge detection using Wikipedia tags and shallow linguistic features. In *Proceedings of the ACL–IJCNLP: Short Papers*, pages 173–176.

Mark Hall, Eibe Frank, Geoffrey Holmes, Bernhard Pfahringer, Peter Reutemann, and Ian H. Witten. 2009. The weka data mining software: An update. *SIGKDD Explorations Newsletter*, 11:10–18.

J. Richard Landis and Gary G. Koch. 1977. The measurement of observer agreement for categorical data. *Biometrics*, 33(1):159–174.

Tim Loughran and Bill McDonald. 2011. When is a liability not a liability? Textual analysis, dictionaries, and 10-Ks. *The Journal of Finance*, 66(1):35–65.

Tim Loughran and Bill McDonald. 2014. Measuring readability in financial disclosures. *The Journal of Finance*, 69(4):1643–1671.

Tim Loughran and Bill McDonald. 2016. Textual analysis in accounting and finance: A survey. *Journal of Accounting Research*, 54(4):1187–1230.

Laurens J. P. van der Maaten and Geoffrey E. Hinton. 2008. Visualizing high-dimensional data using t-SNE. *Journal of Machine Learning Research*, 9:2579–2605.

Tomas Mikolov, Kai Chen, Greg Corrado, and Jeffrey Dean. 2013. Efficient estimation of word representations in vector space. *ArXiv e-prints*.

Saif Mohammed, Bonnie Dorr, and Graeme Hirst. 2008. Computing word-pair antonymy. *Proceedings of the EMNLP*, pages 982–991.

John C. Platt. 1999. Fast training of support vector machines using sequential minimal optimization. In *Advances in Kernel Methods—Support Vector Learning*.

J. Ross Quinlan. 1993. *C4.5: Programs for Machine Learning*. Morgan Kaufmann Publishers, San Francisco.

William Sharpe. 1963. A simplified model for portfolio analysis. *Management Science*, 9:277–293.

Christoph Kilian Theil, Sanja Štajner, Heiner Stuckenschmidt, and Simone Paolo Ponzetto. 2017. Automatic detection of uncertain statements in the financial domain. In *Lecture Notes in Computer Science: Proceedings of the CICLing*, Berlin. Springer. In press.

Ming-Feng Tsai and Chuan-Ju Wang. 2014. Financial keyword expansion via continuous word vector representations. *Proceedings of the EMNLP*, pages 1453–1458.

Sanja Štajner, Goran Glavaš, Simone Paolo Ponzetto, and Heiner Stuckenschmidt. 2017. Domain adaptation for automatic detection of speculative sentences. In *Proceedings of the IEEE ICSC*, pages 164–171.

A Simple End-to-End Question Answering Model for Product Information

Tuan Manh Lai

Adobe Research

tlai@adobe.com

Trung Bui

Adobe Research

bui@adobe.com

Sheng Li

Adobe Research

sheli@adobe.com

Nedim Lipka

Adobe Research

lipka@adobe.com

Abstract

When evaluating a potential product purchase, customers may have many questions in mind. They want to get adequate information to determine whether the product of interest is worth their money. In this paper we present a simple deep learning model for answering questions regarding product facts and specifications. Given a question and a product specification, the model outputs a score indicating their relevance. To train and evaluate our proposed model, we collected a dataset of 7,119 questions that are related to 153 different products. Experimental results demonstrate that — despite its simplicity — the performance of our model is shown to be comparable to a more complex state-of-the-art baseline.

1 Introduction

Customers ask many questions before buying products. Developing a general question answering system to assist customers is challenging, due to the diversity of questions. In this paper, we focus on the task of answering questions regarding product facts and specifications. We formalize the task as follows: Given a question Q about a product P and the list of specifications $(s_1, s_2, ..., s_M)$ of P, the goal is to identify the specification that is most relevant to Q. M is the number of specifications of P, and s_i is the ith specification of P. In this formulation, the task is similar to the answer selection problem (Rao et al., 2016; Bian et al., 2017; Shen et al., 2017). 'Answers' shall be individual product specifications in this case. After identifying the most relevant specification, the final response sentence is generated using predefined templates (Cui et al., 2017). Figure 1 illustrates the overall process.

In this paper, we present a simple deep learning model for selecting the product specification that is most relevant to a given question from a set of candidate specifications. Given a question-specification pair, the model will output a score indicating their relevance. To train and evaluate our model, we collected a dataset of 7,119 questions, covering 153 different products. Despite its simplicity, the performance of our model is shown to be comparable to a more complex state-of-the-art baseline.

2 Related Work

2.1 Answer Selection

Answer selection is an active research field and has drawn a lot of attention. Given a question and a set of candidate answers, the task is to identify which of the candidates contains the correct answer to the question. Two types of deep learning frameworks have been proposed for tackling the answer selection problem. One is the Siamese framework (Bromley et al., 1993) and the other is the Compare-Aggregate framework (Wang et al., 2017; Bian et al., 2017; Shen et al., 2017). In the Siamese framework, the same encoder (e.g., a CNN or a RNN) is used to map each input sentence to a vector representation individually. After that, the final output is determined solely based on the encoded vectors. There is no explicit interaction between the sentences during the encoding process. On the other hand, the Compare-Aggregate framework aims to capture more interactive features between sentences in consideration, therefore typically has better performance when evaluated on public datasets such as TrecQA (Wang et al., 2007) and WikiQA (Yang et al., 2015).

38

Proceedings of the First Workshop on Economics and Natural Language Processing, pages 38–43
Melbourne, Australia, July 20, 2018. ©2018 Association for Computational Linguistics

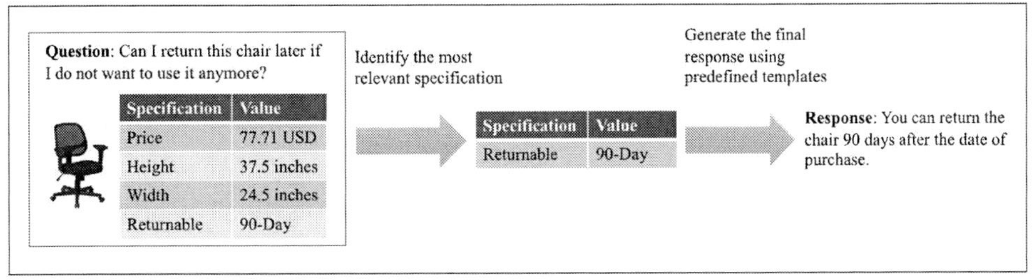

Figure 1: Answering questions regarding product facts and specifications

2.2 Customer Service Chatbot

The most closely related branches of work to ours are probably customer service chatbots for e-commerce websites. An example can be the Shopbot [1] of eBay. Shopbot aims at helping consumers narrow down the best deals from eBays over a billion listings. The bot's main focus is to understand the user intent and then make personalized recommendations. Unlike Shopbot, here we do not focus on making product recommendations. Instead we aim to develop a model for answering questions about product specifications. Another example is the SuperAgent (Cui et al., 2017), a powerful chatbot designed to improve online shopping experience. Given a specific product page and a customer question, SuperAgent selects the best answer from multiple data sources such as in-page product information, existing customer questions & answers, and customer reviews of the product. Even though SuperAgent has a component for answering questions about product specifications, the novelties of our work are: 1) a new simple deep learning model for answering questions about product facts and specifications 2) a new method for collecting data to train and evaluate our model.

3 Model Architecture

Given a question and a set of candidate specifications, the goal is to identify the most relevant specification. We aim to train a classifier that takes a question and a specification name as input and predicts whether the specification is relevant to the question. During inference, given a question, the trained classifier is used to assign a score to every candidate specification based on how relevant the specification is. After that, the top-ranked specification is selected.

A common trait of a number of recent state-of-the-art methods for answer selection is the use of the Compare-Aggregate architecture (Wang et al., 2017; Bian et al., 2017; Shen et al., 2017). Under this architecture, vector representations of smaller units (such as words) of the input sentences are compared. And then the comparison results are aggregated (e.g., by a CNN or a RNN) to determine the relationship of the input sentences. Compared to Siamese models, most Compare-Aggregate models are more complicated and can capture more interactive features between input sentences.

Our task of matching questions and product specifications is similar to the answer selection problem. "Answers" shall be individual product specifications. However, in this case the name of a specification is relatively short. Therefore, our hypothesis is that a well-designed Siamese model would perform as well as a more complicated Compare-Aggregate model. The added complexity of comparing vector representations of smaller units may not be needed as the specification name is already short and descriptive. To this end, we propose a new Siamese model for tackling our problem. We show the overall architecture of our model in Figure 2. Given a question Q and a specification name S, the model calculates a score indicating their relevance through the following layers.

Word Representation Layer. Using word embeddings pre-trained with word2vec (Mikolov et al., 2013) or GloVe (Pennington et al., 2014), we transform Q and S into two sequences $Q_e = [\mathbf{e}_1^Q, \mathbf{e}_2^Q, ..., \mathbf{e}_m^Q]$ and $S_e = [\mathbf{e}_1^S, \mathbf{e}_2^S, ..., \mathbf{e}_n^S]$, where $\mathbf{e}_i^Q$ is the embedding of the ith word of the question and $\mathbf{e}_j^S$ is the embedding of the jth word of the specification name. m and n are the lengths of Q and S, respectively.

BiLSTM Layer. We use a bi-directional

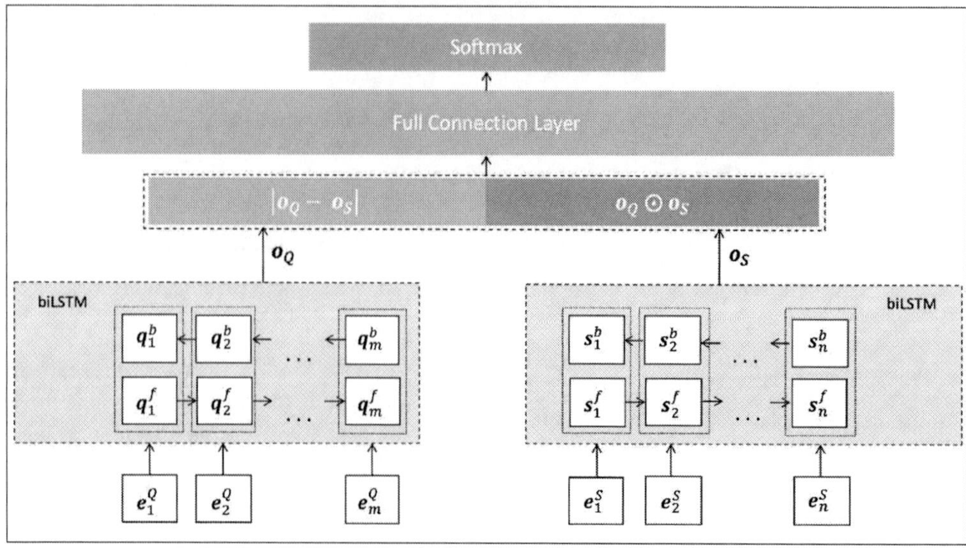

Figure 2: Architecture of our model

LSTM (Hochreiter and Schmidhuber, 1997) to obtain a context-aware vector representation for each position of Q and S. We feed Q_e and S_e individually into a parameter shared bi-directional LSTM model. For the question Q:

$$\mathbf{q}_i^f = \overrightarrow{LSTM}(\mathbf{q}_{i-1}^f, \mathbf{e}_i^Q) \quad i = 1, ..., m$$
$$\mathbf{q}_i^b = \overleftarrow{LSTM}(\mathbf{q}_{i+1}^b, \mathbf{e}_i^Q) \quad i = m, ..., 1$$

where $\mathbf{q}_i^f$ is a vector representation of the first i words in the question (i.e., $[\mathbf{e}_1^Q, \mathbf{e}_2^Q, ..., \mathbf{e}_i^Q]$), $\mathbf{q}_i^b$ is a vector representing the context of the last $m - i + 1$ words in the question (i.e., $[\mathbf{e}_m^Q, \mathbf{e}_{m-1}^Q, ..., \mathbf{e}_i^Q]$). Similarly, we use the same bi-directional LSTM to encode S:

$$\mathbf{s}_j^f = \overrightarrow{LSTM}(\mathbf{s}_{j-1}^f, \mathbf{e}_j^S) \quad j = 1, ..., n$$
$$\mathbf{s}_j^b = \overleftarrow{LSTM}(\mathbf{s}_{j+1}^b, \mathbf{e}_j^S) \quad j = n, ..., 1$$

The context-aware representation at each position of Q or S is obtained by concatenating the two corresponding output sequences from both directions, i.e., $\mathbf{q}_i = \mathbf{q}_i^f \mathbin{\|} \mathbf{q}_i^b$ and $\mathbf{s}_j = \mathbf{s}_j^f \mathbin{\|} \mathbf{s}_j^b$. The final representations of the question and the specification are generated by applying the max-pooling operation on the context-aware representations. We denote the final representation of the question as $\mathbf{o}_Q$ and denote the final representation of the answer as $\mathbf{o}_S$.

Comparison and Output Layers. Following the approach mentioned in (Tai et al., 2015), two feature vectors are calculated from the final encodings $\mathbf{o}_Q$ and $\mathbf{o}_S$: (1) the absolute difference of the two vectors $|\mathbf{o}_Q - \mathbf{o}_S|$; (2) the element-wise multiplication of the two vectors $|\mathbf{o}_Q \odot \mathbf{o}_S|$. The features are then concatenated and fed into a fully connected layer and a softmax layer to produce the final score indicating the probability that specification S is relevant to question Q.

4 Data Collection

The dataset used for experiments is created using Amazon Mechanical Turk (MTurk)[2], an online labor market. MTurk connects requesters (people who have works to be done) and workers (people who work on tasks for money). Requesters can post small tasks for workers to complete for a fee. These small tasks are referred to as HITs or human intelligence tasks. An example of a HIT is finding objects in an image or transcribing an audio file. Requesters have several options for ensuring their HITs are completed in a high-quality manner. Requesters have the opportunity to determine whether to approve completed HITs before having to pay for them. In addition, requesters can also limit which workers are eligible to complete their tasks based on certain criteria.

We crawled the information of products listed in the Home Depot website[3]. For each product, we create HITs where workers are asked to write

---

[2] https://www.mturk.com
[3] https://www.homedepot.com

40

questions regarding the specifications of the product. Figure 3 shows a sample HIT, including the instructions, which are shown to every participated worker. In this sample HIT, a question for the specification "Product Height (in.)" can be "How tall is this shredder?" or "What is the height of this shredder?". To work on the HITs, workers are required to have a 98% HIT approval rate, a minimum of 800 HITs approved, and be located in the United States or Canada. The constraints ensure that the participated workers can provide good questions in English. The final dataset consists of 7,119 question-specification pairs in total, covering 369 kinds of specifications extracted from 153 products. Even though in this work we focus on products listed in the Home Depot website, the data collection process is applicable to other popular e-commerce websites such as Amazon whose product pages typically have a section for product facts and specifications.

5 Experiments and Results

5.1 Training and Evaluation

We set up two different experimental settings. The only difference between the two settings is the way in which we split up the collected HomeDepot dataset into training set, development set, and test set:

1. We divide the dataset so that the test set has no products in common with the training set or the development set.

2. We divide the dataset so that the test set has no specifications in common with the training set or the development set. This is different from the first setting, because two different products may have some specifications in common. For example, a chair and a table usually have a same specification called 'Product Weight'.

In both settings, the proportions of the training set, development set, and test set are roughly 80%, 10%, and 10% of the total questions, respectively.

During training, the objective is to minimize the cross entropy of all question-specification pairs in the training set:

$$loss(\theta) = -log \prod_i p_\theta(y^{(i)}|Q^{(i)}, S^{(i)})$$

where $Q^{(i)}$ and $S^{(i)}$ represent a question-specification pair in the training set, $y^{(i)}$ indicates whether specification $S^{(i)}$ is relevant to question $Q^{(i)}$, and p_θ is the predicted probability with model weights θ. We use all possible question-specification pairs for training. In other words, if there are k questions about a product and the product has h specifications, there are $h \times k$ question-specification examples related to the product, and exactly k of them are positive examples. During testing, for every question about a product, we sort the specifications of the product in descending order based on the predicted probability of being relevant. After that, we calculate the precision at 1 (P@1), precision at 1 (P@2), and precision at 3 (P@3) of our model.

We compare the performance of our model with the unigram model mentioned in (Yu et al., 2014) and the IWAN model proposed in (Shen et al., 2017). The unigram model is a simple bag-of-words model. It first generates a vector representation for each input sentence by summing over the embeddings of all words in the sentence. The final output is then determined based on the generated vector representations. The unigram model is less complicated than our model. On the other hand, the IWAN model belongs to the Compare-Aggregate framework, and it is more sophisticated than our model. In addition to comparing between the fine-grained word representations of the input sentences, the IWAN model also has an inter-weighted layer for evaluating the importance of each word in each sentence. The IWAN model currently achieves state-of-the-art performance on public datasets such as TrecQA (Wang et al., 2007) and WikiQA (Yang et al., 2015).

We make use of the GloVe word embeddings (Pennington et al., 2014) when training the models. We did try the word2vec word embeddings (Mikolov et al., 2013), however they gave worse performances than GloVe. We tune the hyperparameters of each model using the development set.

5.2 Results

Table 1 shows the performances of all the models in the first setting. Table 2 shows the performances of all the models in the second setting. The IWAN model and our model clearly outperform the unigram model. In addition, in both settings, our model's performance is comparable to

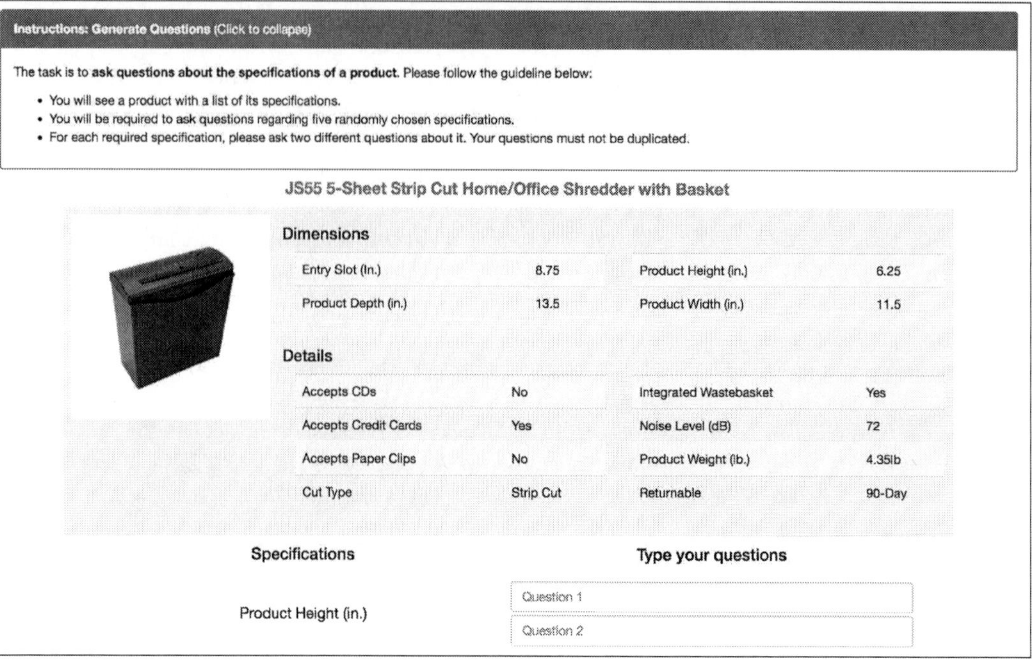

Figure 3: An example of a HIT

Model	P@1	P@2	P@3
Unigram	0.802	0.904	0.927
IWAN	**0.852**	0.927	**0.964**
Our model	0.850	**0.930**	**0.964**

Table 1: Test results in the setting where the test set has no product in common with the training set or the development set

Model	P@1	P@2	P@3
Unigram	0.399	0.529	0.627
IWAN	0.525	**0.661**	**0.789**
Our model	**0.563**	0.640	0.759

Table 2: Test results in the setting where the test set has no specification in common with the training set or the development set

the performance of the IWAN model despite being much simpler. We measured the speeds of our model and the IWAN model. Our proposed model is about 8% faster than the IWAN model. In addition, we see that all models perform worse in the second setting than the first setting. This may due to the fact that in the first setting two different products in the train set and the test set may still have many specifications in common (e.g., a LG TV and a Samsung TV).

6 Conclusion

In this work we explore the task of answering questions related to product facts and specifications. We propose a new, simple deep learning model for tackling the task. To train and evaluate the model, we collected a dataset of question-specification pairs using MTurk. Experimental results show that our model's performance is comparable to a state-of-the-art baseline despite having less complexity. Our proposed model takes less time for training and inference than the state-of-the-art baseline.

Recently, researchers collected a large volume of community question answering data and a large volume of product reviews from the Amazon website (McAuley and Yang, 2016). In the future, we plan to investigate transfer learning techniques to utilize this large dataset for improving the performance of our proposed model.

References

Weijie Bian, Si Li, Zhao Yang, Guang Chen, and Zhiqing Lin. 2017. A compare-aggregate model with dynamic-clip attention for answer selection. In *CIKM*.

Jane Bromley, James W. Bentz, Léon Bottou, Isabelle Guyon, Yann LeCun, Cliff Moore, Eduard Säckinger, and Roopak Shah. 1993. Signature verification using a "siamese" time delay neural network. *IJPRAI*, 7:669–688.

Lei Cui, Shaohan Huang, Furu Wei, Chuanqi Tan, Chaoqun Duan, and Ming Zhou. 2017. Superagent: A customer service chatbot for e-commerce websites. In *ACL*.

Sepp Hochreiter and Jürgen Schmidhuber. 1997. Long short-term memory. *Neural computation*, 9 8:1735–80.

Julian McAuley and Alex Yang. 2016. Addressing complex and subjective product-related queries with customer reviews. In *WWW*.

Tomas Mikolov, Ilya Sutskever, Kai Chen, Greg Corrado, and Jeffrey Dean. 2013. Distributed representations of words and phrases and their compositionality. In *Proceedings of the 26th International Conference on Neural Information Processing Systems - Volume 2*, NIPS'13, pages 3111–3119, USA. Curran Associates Inc.

Jeffrey Pennington, Richard Socher, and Christopher D. Manning. 2014. Glove: Global vectors for word representation. In *EMNLP*.

Jinfeng Rao, Hua He, and Jimmy J. Lin. 2016. Noise-contrastive estimation for answer selection with deep neural networks. In *CIKM*.

Gehui Shen, Yunlun Yang, and Zhi-Hong Deng. 2017. Inter-weighted alignment network for sentence pair modeling. In *EMNLP*.

Kai Sheng Tai, Richard Socher, and Christopher D. Manning. 2015. Improved semantic representations from tree-structured long short-term memory networks. *CoRR*, abs/1503.00075.

Mengqiu Wang, Noah A. Smith, and Teruko Mitamura. 2007. What is the jeopardy model? a quasi-synchronous grammar for qa. In *EMNLP-CoNLL*.

Zhiguo Wang, Wael Hamza, and Radu Florian. 2017. Bilateral multi-perspective matching for natural language sentences. In *IJCAI*.

Yi Yang, Scott Wen-tau Yih, and Chris Meek. 2015. Wikiqa: A challenge dataset for open-domain question answering. ACL Association for Computational Linguistics.

Lei Yu, Karl Moritz Hermann, Phil Blunsom, and Stephen G. Pulman. 2014. Deep learning for answer sentence selection. *CoRR*, abs/1412.1632.

Sentence Classification for Investment Rules Detection

Youness Mansar and **Sira Ferradans**
Fortia Financial Solutions
17 av. George V, Paris
France
`name.surname@fortia.fr`

Abstract

In the last years, compliance requirements for the banking sector have greatly augmented, making the current compliance processes difficult to maintain. Any process that allows to accelerate the identification and implementation of compliance requirements can help address this issues. The contributions of the paper are twofold: we propose a new NLP task that is the investment rule detection, and a group of methods identify them. We show that the proposed methods are highly performing and fast, thus can be deployed in production.

1 Introduction

Compliance requirements have augmented dramatically in the last years, specially in the financial sector. Investment funds are obliged by law to publish their investment strategy at a very detailed level. If the fund does not follow precisely these rules, it will be fined by the corresponding regulatory institution. According to Thomson Reuters there were regulatory changes every 12 minutes, on average per day in 2015 (Thomson Reuters, 2015). But, it takes months to implement every regulatory change, thus, any process that allows to spot regulatory changes can help accelerate this updating process. This is important since if an investment fund does not follow precisely these rules, it will be fined by the corresponding regulatory institution. In fact, in the last years, the income dedicated to fines and settlements has increased by almost 45x for the biggest EU and US banks (Kaminski and Robu, 2016).

The compliance department of Depositary banks are in charge of controlling that these rules are actually followed. In order to avoid sanctions, they define a 4-eye protocol for rule identification. This protocol consists in having two or more people read and highlight the investment rules of the prospectus of each investment fund they control. Once two people have highlighted the same prospectus, a third person introduces all the rules in the system. Identifying the rules is time consuming and tedious. This process takes days for human actors, we propose a method that takes seconds thanks to the use of machine learning. Although other methods have acknowledged the importance of having the rules isolated (Cashman et al., 2002; Beale, 2004), the current systems assume that the rules have already been identified and translated into executable code.

In this paper, we propose to detect investment rules using binary classification of sentences. In section 2, we present the state of the art in sentence classification. In section 3.1, we give all the details on the data and the posed problem. The proposed solutions are given in section 3.2 and the obtained results in section 3.3. Section 4 concludes the paper and gives future work. [1]

2 Related Works

Sentence Classification. Sentence classification is a classic research area in natural language processing. Approaches previous to 2010 focus mostly on the extraction of document meaning through representative features that would be used as input to classic machine learning algorithms, such as SVM, knn, or Naive Bayes (see (Khan et al., 2010) for a review on the topic). The rise of Deep Learning techniques impacts also the sentence classification literature, appearing methods based on CNNs. More specifically, a modification of (Collobert et al., 2011) was proposed by

---

[1] **Note:** There is a Patent Pending for the presented approach. It was submitted the 18 December 2017 at the EPO and has the number EP17306801

Proceedings of the First Workshop on Economics and Natural Language Processing, pages 44–48
Melbourne, Australia, July 20, 2018. ©2018 Association for Computational Linguistics

Kim (Kim, 2014), showing how a simple model together with pre-trained word representations can be highly performing. But the use of word-embeddings has been challenged for CNNs, (Johnson and Zhang, 2014, 2015) propose a semi-supervised setting that allows to learn a small text-region representation. Zhang et al. (Zhang et al., 2015) propose a CNN based directly on character representations, without explicitly encoding words. CNNs are highly dependent on the window size, (Lai et al., 2015; Visin et al., 2015) propose the use of Recurrent Convolutional Neural Networks to overcome this issue. (Guggilla et al., 2016) propose the use of LSTMs for classification of online user comments. In order to avoid problems due to lack of data, (Liu et al., 2016) propose multitask learning using LSTMs.

Word embeddings. The lack of big databases with tagged data is a common problem for Deep Learning models. Collobert *et al.* (Collobert et al., 2011) empirically proved the usefulness of using unsupervised word representations for a variety of different NLP tasks and since then, it is widely accepted that, for small and middle size databases (< 10k samples), the use of word embeddings improves the final results. *Word embeddings* is the name associated to a group of language model methods that map words into a vector space. Introduced by Bengio et al. (Bengio et al., 2003), the authors proposed a statistical language model based on shallow neural networks. The goal was to predict the following word, given the previous context in the sentence, showing a major advance with respect to n-grams. Collobert *et al.* (Collobert et al., 2011) set the neural network architecture for many current approaches. Mikolov *et al.* (Mikolov et al., 2013) proposed a simplified model (`word2vec`) that allows to train on larger corpora. They also show how semantic relationships emerge from this training. Pennignton *et al.* (Pennington et al., 2014), GloVe, maintain the semantic capacity of word2vec while introducing the statistical information from latent semantic analysis (LSA) showing that they can improve in semantic and syntactic tasks.

3 Rule detection in prospectus

In this section we present the problem of *rule detection* in investment fund prospectus, and our proposal for tackling it.

3.1 The data

Investment fund prospectus are papers where the fund informs the regulatory institution and its future clients of its investment strategy, its risk management, the company structure, etc. Most of these documents are publicly available in the regulation authority web page, see for instance for French documents (AMF, 2018). The investment rules that we want to identify are very precise rules which can be of different kinds, and, in general, very different from other sentences in the same text as can be observed in Table 1.

The Gold standard database. The data used in the supervised part of the model is around 3.5k annotated sentences for each language (English and French). The sentences were split into two classes, the label 1 is used for rules and 0 is used for non rules, as shown in Table 1.

3.2 Proposed methods

In this subsection we detail the proposed algorithms. The task required multiple pre-processing steps that are used for data preparation before training or inference. The first step is to segment the document into a list of sentence then each sentence is tokenized into multiple elements based mostly on space and punctuation characters. Each token is then mapped to a unique id in order to produce a list of integer from each sentence which then will be fed to the regression model.

Word embeddings. The word vector values are initialized using the GloVe algorithm Pennignton *et al.* (Pennington et al., 2014) and then fine-tuned along with the model regression parameters during training. We used a corpus of fund prospectuses and wikipedia pages to train a domain-specific word embedding. This is justified by the fact that some words used in prospectuses are uncommon in the general use of language and thus are not included in available word vectors pre-trained on Wikipedia or common crawl alone.

3.2.1 Linear network model

The Linear network model in this case is a logistic regression applied to an un-weighted average of dense word vectors. The advantage of this model is that it is simple while it also takes advantage of the unsupervised pre-training of the word embeddings. This also means that is very fast and computationally cheap compared to other models

Sentence	Tag
The Fund will invest at least 70% of its net assets in sub investment grade corporate debt securities with a credit rating equivalent to BB+ or lower and denominated in USD.	1
The SICAV may invest in OTC markets.	1
The Company may not invest in gold, spot commodities, or real estate	1
The management fee is 0.1%	0
The asset manager JP Morgan assigns BNP Security Services as its depositary bank.	0

Table 1: Examples of sentences in the Data base.

presented here. In Figure 1, we can see the overall architecture of the model.

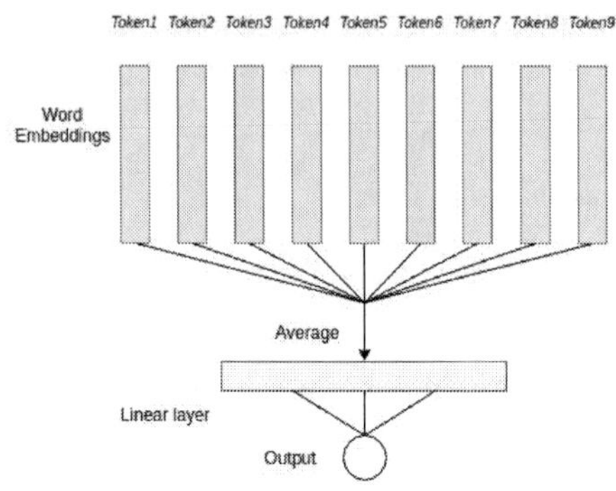

Figure 1: Linear Network architecture

3.2.2 Convolutional Neural Network

We used a CNN architecture similar to the one introduced in (Kim, 2014). It consists of the following layers:

- Convolutional Layer : Three 1-dimensional convolution layers applied in parallel to the input embedding sequence. Each convolution layer uses a different filter size $\{3, 4, 5\}$ and captures sentence information at different scales (3-gram, 4-gram, 5-gram). The convolution filters learn translation-invariant representations which is useful for language because it allows for weight sharing between neurons and thus reduces significantly the number of weights compared to a fully connected layer. We use 100 filters for each layer and ReLu as a non-linearity for the convolution layers.

- Max-pooling : Applies a max operation across the sequence and returns an output that

has the same size as the number of filters in each convolution layer.

- Concat Layer : Concatenates the output of each Max-pooling together.

- Linear Layer : Applies a linear mapping from the concat layer to the output.

- Sigmoid Activation : Maps the output to the [0,1] range.

In Figure 2, we can see the overall architecture of the model.

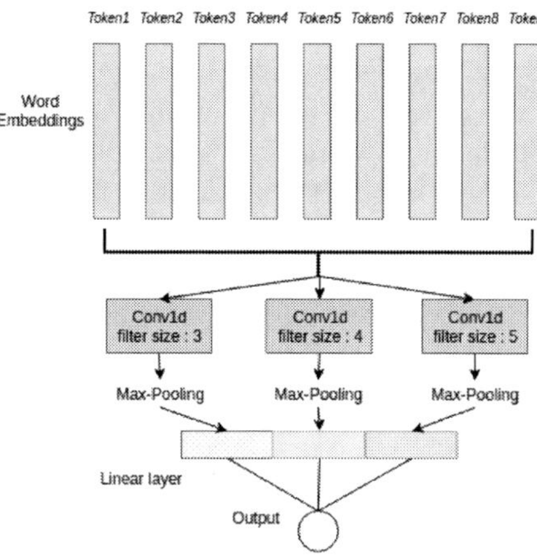

Figure 2: CNN architecture

3.2.3 Bi-directional Long-Short-Term-Memory

The Bi-LSTM model was first introduced in (Graves and Schmidhuber, 2005). Here, we used a specific model that consists of the following Layers :

- Forward LSTM : Sequential layer that is applied to the list of word embeddings from the first token in the sentence to the last token and outputs the lstm cell state of the last token of the sentence.

- Backward LSTM : Sequential layer that is applied to the list of word embeddings from the last token in the sentence to the first token and outputs the lstm cell state of the first token of the sentence.

- Concat Layer : Concatenates the output of each LSTM layer.

- Linear Layer : Applies a linear mapping from the concat layer to the output.

- Sigmoid Activation : Maps the output to the [0,1] range.

In Figure 3, we can see the overall architecture of the model.

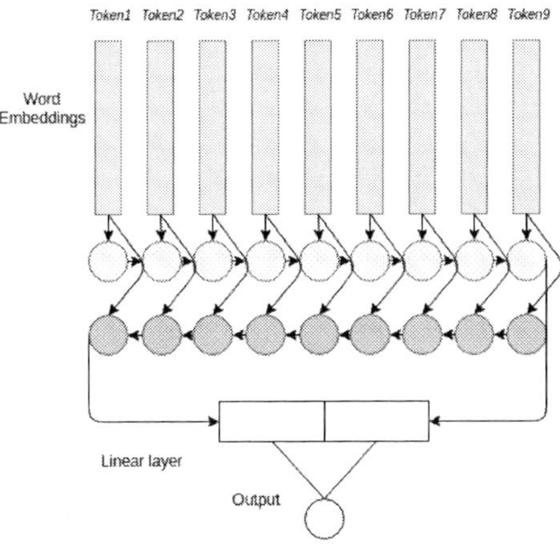

Figure 3: LSTM architecture

3.2.4 Implementation details

We used Keras (Chollet et al., 2015) with Tensor-Flow Backend throughout our experiments.
We use Adadelta (Zeiler, 2012) Optimizer with a learning rate of 0.001 and a batch-size of 50.
A Dropout (Srivastava et al., 2014) of 0.5 is used after the concat layer for LSTM and CNN and after the average layer for the Linear network model for regularization.
We used Binary Cross-entropy in all the models losses.

3.3 Results

We present a performance comparison of the architectures described above both in terms of accuracy/Precision/recall but also in terms of inference time as it is a also an important metric to consider when deploying a model in a production environment.

Model	Acc (std)	P (std)	R (std)
Linear	88.2(1.5)	88.2(3.3)	73.5(3.5)
CNN	**93.7**(1.0)	**90.8**(2.6)	**89.7**(3.8)
Bi-LSTM	93.3(1.1)	90.5(3.0)	88.8(2.7)

Table 2: French 10-fold Cross-validation results

Model	Acc (std)	P (std)	R (std)
Linear	87.7(3.5)	83.3(4.1)	60.8(1.4)
CNN	**94.3**(1.4)	**90.4**(4.2)	**85.8**(2.3)
Bi-LSTM	93.7(1.1)	88.8(1.9)	84.7(5.3)

Table 3: English 10-fold Cross-validation results

The convolutional model seem to yield slightly better results on average compared to the Bi-LSTM which is in line with the results presented in (Guggilla et al., 2016). Both Bi-LSTM and CNN outperform the linear network model because they take into account the order of tokens in the sentence while the linear network model does not.

Model	Time per sample (s)
Linear	$1.2e^{-4}$
CNN	$3.1e^{-4}$
Bi-LSTM	$1.8e^{-3}$

Table 4: Inference Time performance comparison

Because of its simplicity the linear network model is the fastest out of the three and the Bi-LSTM is 6 times slower than the CNN while giving worse results.

4 Conclusions and further work

We have presented a method to detect and isolate mandatory rules in regulatory documents. The objective is to automate the detection of investment rule in prospectuses using a classifier. This helps compliance experts avoid the tedious work of reading documents that are sometimes as long as 500 pages and take days to read in order to select very few sentences.

We described the frameworks used, the pre-processing steps and compared multiple classification models in terms of Accuracy/Precision/Recall and inference time. The results show that convolutional neural networks have the best trade-off between accuracy and execution time and are thus the best model for this task.

References

AMF. 2018. Geco database. `http://geco.amf-france.org/Bio/rech_opcvm.aspx`. Online, accessed: 2018-04-18.

N.C.L. Beale. 2004. System and method for generating compliance rules for trading systems. `https://www.google.com/patents/EP0990215B1?cl=en`. EP Patent 0,990,215.

Yoshua Bengio, Réjean Ducharme, Pascal Vincent, and Christian Jauvin. 2003. A neural probabilistic language model. *Journal of machine learning research* 3(Feb):1137–1155.

D. Cashman, D. Damphousse, V. Drysdale, L. Ekhtman, C. Guerriero, K. Hebert, R. Kumar, R. Leeper, H. Levine, B. Mandel, et al. 2002. Systeme de gestion de fonds financiers et de conformite aux directives en matiere d'investissement de portefeuille. `https://www.google.com/patents/EP1212711A1?cl=fr`. EP Patent App. EP20,000,921,568.

François Chollet et al. 2015. Keras. `https://keras.io`.

Ronan Collobert, Jason Weston, Léon Bottou, Michael Karlen, Koray Kavukcuoglu, and Pavel Kuksa. 2011. Natural language processing (almost) from scratch. *Journal of Machine Learning Research* 12(Aug):2493–2537.

Alex Graves and Jürgen Schmidhuber. 2005. Framewise phoneme classification with bidirectional lstm and other neural network architectures. *Neural Networks* 18(5-6):602–610.

Chinnappa Guggilla, Tristan Miller, and Iryna Gurevych. 2016. Cnn-and lstm-based claim classification in online user comments. In *Proceedings of COLING 2016, the 26th International Conference on Computational Linguistics: Technical Papers*. pages 2740–2751.

Rie Johnson and Tong Zhang. 2014. Effective use of word order for text categorization with convolutional neural networks. *arXiv preprint arXiv:1412.1058* .

Rie Johnson and Tong Zhang. 2015. Semi-supervised convolutional neural networks for text categorization via region embedding. In *Advances in neural information processing systems*. pages 919–927.

Piotr Kaminski and Kate Robu. 2016. A best practice model for bank compliance. http://www.mckinsey.com/business-functions/risk/our-insights/a-best-practice-model-for-bank-compliance.

Aurangzeb Khan, Baharum Baharudin, Lam Hong Lee, and Khairullah Khan. 2010. A review of machine learning algorithms for text-documents classification. *Journal of advances in information technology* 1(1):4–20.

Yoon Kim. 2014. Convolutional neural networks for sentence classification. *arXiv preprint arXiv:1408.5882* .

Siwei Lai, Liheng Xu, Kang Liu, and Jun Zhao. 2015. Recurrent convolutional neural networks for text classification. In *AAAI*. volume 333, pages 2267–2273.

Pengfei Liu, Xipeng Qiu, and Xuanjing Huang. 2016. Recurrent neural network for text classification with multi-task learning. *arXiv preprint arXiv:1605.05101* .

Tomas Mikolov, Kai Chen, Greg Corrado, and Jeffrey Dean. 2013. Efficient estimation of word representations in vector space. *arXiv preprint arXiv:1301.3781* .

Jeffrey Pennington, Richard Socher, and Christopher D Manning. 2014. GloVe: Global vectors for word representation. In *Proceedings of EMNLP 2014*. volume 14, pages 1532–43.

Nitish Srivastava, Geoffrey Hinton, Alex Krizhevsky, Ilya Sutskever, and Ruslan Salakhutdinov. 2014. Dropout: A simple way to prevent neural networks from overfitting. *J. Mach. Learn. Res.* 15(1):1929–1958. http://dl.acm.org/citation.cfm?id=2627435.2670313.

Financial & Risk Thomson Reuters. 2015. Risk management: Turn regulatory compliance into a business opportunity. `https://financial.thomsonreuters.com/en/markets-industries/risk-management-tools.html?utm_campaign=e4&utm_medium=social&utm_source=FRblog&utm_content=DCraigPeakRegulatory`.

Francesco Visin, Kyle Kastner, Kyunghyun Cho, Matteo Matteucci, Aaron Courville, and Yoshua Bengio. 2015. Renet: A recurrent neural network based alternative to convolutional networks. *arXiv preprint arXiv:1505.00393* .

Matthew D. Zeiler. 2012. Adadelta: An adaptive learning rate method. *CoRR* abs/1212.5701.

Xiang Zhang, Junbo Zhao, and Yann LeCun. 2015. Character-level convolutional networks for text classification. In *Advances in neural information processing systems*. pages 649–657.

Leveraging News Sentiment to Improve Microblog Sentiment Classification in the Financial Domain

Tobias Daudert, Paul Buitelaar, Sapna Negi
Insight Centre for Data Analytics, Data Science Institute, National University of Ireland, Galway
`firstname.lastname@insight-centre.org`

Abstract

With the rising popularity of social media in the society and in research, analysing texts short in length, such as microblogs, becomes an increasingly important task. As a medium of communication, microblogs carry peoples sentiments and express them to the public. Given that sentiments are driven by multiple factors including the news media, the question arises if the sentiment expressed in news and the news article themselves can be leveraged to detect and classify sentiment in microblogs. Prior research has highlighted the impact of sentiments and opinions on the market dynamics, making the financial domain a prime case study for this approach. Therefore, this paper describes ongoing research dealing with the exploitation of news contained sentiment to improve microblog sentiment classification in a financial context.

1 Introduction

In an increasingly complex world in which information is almost instantly available and flows with nearly no limits, people are facing a magnitude of information not always objective or unbiased. Especially with the increasing popularity of Twitter, short texts dense in information and usually rich in sentiment are becoming increasingly relevant when it comes to the education of people through news stories (Mitchell and Page, 2015). In 2017, close to 23% of the people worldwide preferred social media as the selected gateway to digital news content. The importance of digital news is also emphasized by the increasing amount of time per day that adults in the U.S. spent with digital media which grew from 214 to 353 minutes

in the last 6 years. Within the same period, the amount of time adults spent with traditional media decreased from 453 to 360 minutes. However, traditional news are still important and at minimum as influential as digital media; in 2017, 32% of the people worldwide accessed digital news directly on a news website[1][2].

Given the importance of both news sources (i.e. microblogs and news stories), their similar instantaneous availability, and their topic intersections, it becomes relevant to study how news articles and microblogs affect each other and, in more detail, how the sentiments contained in both affect each other. This paper presents ongoing research which is dealing with this question and utilises the news-contained sentiment to improve microblog sentiment classification. This research is built on the hypothesis that sentiment carried in news articles will eventually affect the sentiment expressed in microblogs (e.g. a person develops an opinion after reading a news article and later utilises microblogs to express it).

2 Background

As the world gets increasingly connected, factors affecting peoples' sentiment rise. Research has shown the link between sentiments and the market dynamics making the financial domain an important area for sentiment analysis in text (Van De Kauter et al., 2015; Kearney and Liu, 2014). Sentiments are contained in multiple forms of text, such as news and microblogs. News can convey information regarding macroeconomic factors, company-specific reports, or political information, which can be relevant to the market

---

[1] `https://www.statista.com/statistics/565628/time-spent-digital-traditional-media-usa/`
[2] `https://www.statista.com/chart/10262/selected-gateways-to-digital-news-content/`

49

Proceedings of the First Workshop on Economics and Natural Language Processing, pages 49–54
Melbourne, Australia, July 20, 2018. ©2018 Association for Computational Linguistics

(Sinha, 2014). Good news tend to lift markets and increase optimism, bad news tend to lower markets (Schuster, 2003; Van De Kauter et al., 2015). Not only news are an important factor for the markets. In 2011, Bollen et al. (2011) showed that changes in public mood reflect value shifts in the Dow Jones Industrial Index three to four days later. Therefore, analysing financial text becomes progressively important and research is shifting its attention towards this topic. An example, is the Semeval 2017 Task 5 which focused on fine-grained sentiment analysis on financial microblogs in subtask 1, and news headlines in subtask 2. Given the relevance and availability of microblogs and news, both are an intriguing source for sentiment analysis. Although the existing interest in media-expressed sentiment, most of the research focuses on news, particularly news titles (i.e headlines) (Nassirtoussi et al., 2014; Kearney and Liu, 2014). This is due to three reasons, 1) annotating news titles requires less effort than full articles; 2) news titles summarise the main points of the news article, thus, it should reflect the article's content (Peramunetilleke and Wong, 2002; Huang et al., 2010); and 3) news titles are written in a way to attract readers' attention, hence, having a high load of emotional and sentimental content (Strapparava and Mihalcea, 2007; Meyer et al., 2017; Corcoran, 2006). Despite the growing attention to the sentiment classification of news, and news headlines in specific, datasets dealing with financial news titles are still rare; especially regarding a fine-grained classification in contrast to only polarity. Overall, common sources for sentiment analysis are K-10 fillings, news articles, and microblogs. A dataset linking microblogs to news articles is not existing, to the best of our knowledge. Thus far, no work investigated financial sentiments further, excluding creating new data sets, lexicons, and rule lists and applying them to retrieve better sentiment classifications.

Approaches for sentiment analysis can be grouped into knowledge-based techniques and statistical methods. Although easily accessible, knowledge-based techniques are hindered by their inability to correctly interpret semantics and nuanced concepts (Cambria et al., 2017). In the case of the statistical methods, common approaches include support vector machines (SVM) and artificial neural networks (ANN). In parallel with the momentum of artificial neural networks, the types of classifiers used in the area of sentiment analysis are shifting. While Nassirtoussi et al. (2014) report on a vast majority of the literature using SVMs and scarcely ANNs, participants of the 2017 Semeval task 5 (Cortis et al., 2017) have substantially used ANNs as well as other deep learning approaches such as Recurrent Neural Networks or Convolution Neural Networks. Artificial neural networks are powerful in terms of prediction accuracy and offer a high flexibility; however, they are arguably the least transparent models (Strumbelj et al., 2010). As interpretability comes at the cost of flexibility, accuracy, or efficiency (Ribeiro et al., 2016), the consideration of the trade-off between classifier types becomes essential. This is notably the case for automated trading and medical diagnosis (Caruana et al., 2015) where the application of a "black box" algorithm can pose a significant risk. Although potentially less powerful, machine learning approaches based on simpler algorithms allow for the identification of the components responsible for the achieved prediction.

This work is inspired by the proposal described in Daudert (2017); specifically, it exploits the idea of utilising a combination of multiple sentiments. Our work conducts the first step into a new direction by focusing on the achievement of a superior sentiment classification trough the exploitation of the relations between different sentiments.

3 Methodology

The methodology implemented in this work is based on two foundations: the creation of a suitable dataset and its use in a Machine Learning (ML) prediction model.

The dataset is a vital component of this research. As the goal is to leverage relations of sentiments in both data types, news and microblogs, a dataset linking and combining both data is compulsory. Due to its novelty, it became necessary to choose a microblog dataset and then create a novel complimentary news dataset covering the same period and entities. With these complementary datasets, the following step consisted in linking them, enriching the pre-existing microblog dataset with 1) information regarding the related news for each microblog, and 2) the related-news sentiment.

The ML algorithm chosen for this task is a Support Vector Machine (SVM). This SVM is trained and tested with the datasets explicitly created for this work, with the aim of exploring whether news-

Minimum	Maximum	Average	Total
1	40	6.4	106

Table 1: Number of news in dataset MRN per entity. News articles can cover more than one entity.

Type	Dataset M	Subset A	Subset B
Training	1990	370	221
Test	498	93	56
Total	2488	463	277

Table 2: Number of microblogs per dataset.

contained sentiment can bring an advantage to microblog sentiment classification. To investigate this, we compare a classification purely based on the microblog messages with a classification based on microblog messages as well as news sentiment.

3.1 Data

This research makes use of two datasets; an existing microblog dataset and a novel news dataset created for this work. On one hand, it utilises the microblog dataset (M) from the Semeval 2017 Task 5 - subtask 1 (Cortis et al., 2017). This dataset contains 2,488 microblogs retrieved from Twitter[3] collected between March 11th and 18th 2016 as well as StockTwits[4]. Particularly, the dataset contains the microblog message, source, as well as a manually assigned cashtag (e.g. '$AAPL' for Apple Inc), span, and continuous sentiment score. On the other hand, the newly created microblogs-related news dataset (MRN) consists of 106 news, specifically, it contains the news' titles, urls, time and date, a sentiment score, and, if available, a description for each news. The news data was gathered from multiple sources such as `wsj.com` or `bloomberg.com`.

To be selected for this dataset, two criteria have to be satisfied to ensure the relatedness to dataset M. (1) Only news published between March 11th and 18th 2016 have been considered, and (2) each news has to deal with at least one company mentioned in dataset M. To fulfill the second criteria, we automatically extracted all 871 distinct cashtags from dataset M and used those to retrieve the respective company names using Stocktwits. With this list of cashtags and the associated company names, all news have been filtered and only news containing at least one of the 871 cashtags

and/or company names have been kept. Overall, the MRN dataset covers 18 unique entities in 463 microblogs. Further information is given in Table 1.

In the following step, all news in MRN have been annotated with a sentiment score. The dataset was presented to two annotators who assigned, based on title and description, a sentiment score within the five classes [-1.0, -0.5, 0.0, 0.5, 1.0], with 0.0 as neutral. In cases when the two annotators did not agree on a particular sentiment score, an expert decided the most appropriate rating. The inter-annotator agreement on all classes achieved a Cohen's Kappa coefficient of 0.52; when using an aggregation of 3 classes [-1.0, 0.0, 1.0] it achieved a value of 0.61.

Preliminary experiments have shown that the datasets were too small to achieve adequate results on a continuous sentiment scale, thus, it became necessary to increase the data per class and decrease the possible number of classes. Therefore, sentiment scores in dataset M have been processed to cluster data in three classes by transforming sentiment scores above and lower 0.0. Scores larger than 0.0 became 1.0; sentiment score smaller than 0.0 became -1.0.

3.2 Assigning a News Sentiment to Microblogs

With the knowledge that all news in dataset MRN are dealing with companies covered by a minimum of one microblog in dataset M, a question is raised on how to convey the news-contained sentiment to each microblog. We choose an entity based approach and assume that within a certain period, sentiments regarding the same entity should be similar across different data sources. Therefore, one news sentiment was calculated for each entity mentioned in dataset MRN. The sentiments for all news dealing with the same entity have been added together and then divided by the total number of news dealing with this entity.

Although each news in dataset MRN is linked to at least one microblog in dataset M, not all microblogs have a relation to at least one news. Dataset MRN covers 18 unique entities whereas dataset M covers 871 unique entities. Thus, we created two subsets of dataset M according to the microblogs' relation to dataset MRN (Table 2). Subset A contains all microblogs (from Twitter and Stocktwits) which have a relation to at least

---

	Subset A		Subset B	
Measure \ Features	MT	MT & NS	MT	MT & NS
Micro F1-Score	0.7097	**0.7312**	0.7321	**0.75**
Macro F1-Score	0.7874	**0.8055**	0.651	**0.6938**
Weighted F1-Score	0.6997	**0.7244**	0.7111	**0.7406**
Euclidean Distance	10.3923	**10**	7.746	**7.4833**
Mean Error Squared	1.1613	**1.0753**	1.0714	**1**

Table 3: Scores as obtained by the SVM model for subset A and subset B. MT abbreviates the message text, and NS the news sentiment.

Measure \ Features	MT	MT & NS-3
Micro F1-Score	0.7711	**0.7731**
Macro F1-Score	0.493	**0.4948**
Weighted F1-Score	0.76035	**0.7626**
Euclidean Distance	20.8567	**20.7605**
Mean Error Squared	0.8735	**0.8655**

Table 4: Scores obtained by the SVM model for dataset M. MT abbreviates the message text, and NS-3 the news sentiment aggregated into the 3 classes [-1.0, 0.0, 1.0].

one news (e.g. the same entities are present in both the microblog and the news article); subset B contains only the microblogs from Twitter which have a relation to at least one news. Subset B is necessary as the stocktwits were not specifically collected in the same period as the tweets. All three datasets have been randomised and split into a training set of 80% and a test set of 20% to avoid any bias from the structure of the Semeval data.

3.3 Preprocessing the Data

To prepare the textual data for the ML model, the following preprocessing steps were performed:

1. URLs were replaced with $< url >$

2. Numbers were replaced with $< number >$

3. With $WORD$ representing the original hastag:

    (a) hastags in upper case were replaced with $< hashtag > WORD < allcaps >$

    (b) the remaining cases were replaced with $< hashtag > WORD$

4. Smileys and emoticons were replaced with a description (e.g.☺ becomes $slightly\_smiling\_face$)[5]

The processed text was then transformed into an unigram tf-idf representation.

[5]http://www.unicode.org/emoji/charts/
full-emoji-list.html

3.4 Experimental Setup

The experiments use a SVM employing a linear kernel. This decision was made based on the approaches of the best teams at the Semeval 2017 Task 5 - Subtask 1. LiblinearSVC was chosen for this task (Pedregosa et al., 2012). The performance is evaluated using F1-Scores, the Euclidean distance, and the mean error squared. The SVM model is trained and tested in two distinct approaches: (1) a feature matrix representing the microblogs' messages; (2) a feature matrix representing the microblogs' messages enriched with the assigned news sentiment for each microblog. The default settings were employed, except for the maximum number of iterations which is decreased to 500 and the random state which is set to 42.

4 Results

Table 3 presents the classification results on subset A and subset B. As the table shows, utilising the news sentiment improves all measures. The weighted F1-Score for subset A is increased by 3.51% and the Euclidean distance is decreased by 7.4%; for subset B the F1-Score increases by 4.15% and the Euclidean distance is decreased by 6.66%. This suggests that the news sentiment is benefiting the classification. Applying this classification on dataset M shows similar results (Table 4). Although, it is containing unrelated stocktwits collected at a different period, and having only 18.6% of the microblogs with an assigned news sentiment, all measures improve; the weighted F1-Score improves 0.3% and the Euclidean distance 0.46%. However, for dataset M, it is important to notice that to make a measurable difference, the news sentiments have been aggregated into the 3 classes [-1.0, 0.0, 1.0].

5   Conclusion and Future Work

This paper presents novel research leveraging news-contained sentiment to improve microblog sentiment classification. As there are no existing datasets for this task, we created a new dataset linking microblogs and news. Our current experiments show an improvement in sentiment classification across all used measures. This insight has the potential to change the future of sentiment analysis, shifting the focus from creating continuously larger datasets to cross-data linked approaches exploiting knowledge across multiple data types. In this work, we use manually annotated news sentiment to show its impact on microblog sentiment classification. Future works must consider the quality of automated news sentiment retrieval, therefore, identifying a threshold which determines whether news sentiment has an impact on microblog sentiment classification or not. Although the promising results, tangible points for improvement exist in the limited size of the dataset as well as the noise in the data. The microblog dataset applied is outdated by two years which hindered the retrieval of relevant news stories. Moreover, it contains messages unrelated to any event identified within the news; this is predominant for the stocktwits which were not collected within a defined period. Therefore, an important future contribution is the creation of a larger dataset, limited to a given period and ideally covering the same entities. Considering the linking of news and microblogs, we believe that more sophisticated approaches beyond the occurrence of identical entities will increase the impact of news sentiment on microblog sentiment classification. News and microblogs might deal with the same company but cover different topics which are not significantly related. Furthermore, this work does not consider the importance of the news articles' source; sources with a higher credibility might be more influential than others.
Although this study is not sufficiently exhaustive

to provide a conclusive answer of the benefit of incorporating news-contained sentiment for microblog sentiment classification, it suggests the potential of leveraging knowledge from across multiple data sources and builds the foundation for upcoming research in the field of sentiment analysis.

Acknowledgments

This work has been supported by Science Foundation Ireland under grant number SFI/12/RC/2289

References

Johan Bollen, Huina Mao, and Xiaojun Zeng. 2011. Twitter mood predicts the stock market. *Journal of Computational Science*, 2(1):1–8.

Erik Cambria, Dipankar Das, Sivaji Bandyopadhyay, and Antonio Feraco. 2017. Affective Computing and Sentiment Analysis. In *A Practical Guide to Sentiment Analysis*, pages 1–10.

Rich Caruana, Yin Lou, Johannes Gehrke, Paul Koch, Marc Sturm, and Noemie Elhadad. 2015. Intelligible Models for HealthCare. In *Proceedings of the 21th ACM SIGKDD International Conference on Knowledge Discovery and Data Mining - KDD '15*, pages 1721–1730, New York, New York, USA. ACM Press.

Paul Corcoran. 2006. Emotional Framing in Australian Journalism. *Australian & New Zealand Communication Association International Conference*.

Keith Cortis, Andre Freitas, Tobias Daudert, Manuela Huerlimann, Manel Zarrouk, Siegfried Handschuh, and Brian Davis. 2017. SemEval-2017 Task 5: Fine-Grained Sentiment Analysis on Financial Microblogs and News. *Proceedings of the 11th International Workshop on Semantic Evaluation (SemEval-2017)*, pages 519–535.

Tobias Daudert. 2017. Analysing Market Sentiments: Utilising Deep Learning to Exploit Relationships within the Economy. In *Proceedings of the Student Research Workshop associated with RANLP 2017*, pages 10–16, Varna, Bulgaria.

Chenn Jung Huang, Jia Jian Liao, Dian Xiu Yang, Tun Yu Chang, and Yun Cheng Luo. 2010. Realization of a news dissemination agent based on weighted association rules and text mining techniques. *Expert Systems with Applications*, 37(9):6409–6413.

Colm Kearney and Sha Liu. 2014. Textual sentiment in finance: A survey of methods and models. *International Review of Financial Analysis*, 33:171–185.

Bradley Meyer, Marwan Bikdash, and Xiangfeng Dai. 2017. Fine-grained financial news sentiment analysis. *Conference Proceedings - IEEE SOUTHEAST-CON*.

Amy Mitchell and Dana Page. 2015. The Evolving Role of News on Twitter and Facebook. Technical report, pewresearch.org.

Arman Khadjeh Nassirtoussi, Saeed Aghabozorgi, Teh Ying Wah, and David Chek Ling Ngo. 2014. Text mining for market prediction: A systematic review. *Expert Systems with Applications*, 41(16):7653–7670.

Fabian Pedregosa, Gal Varoquaux, Alexandre Gramfort, Vincent Michel, Bertrand Thirion, Olivier Grisel, Mathieu Blondel, Peter Prettenhofer, Ron Weiss, Vincent Dubourg, Jake Vanderplas, Alexandre Passos, David Cournapeau, Matthieu Brucher, Matthieu Perrot, and douard Duchesnay. 2012. Scikit-learn: Machine Learning in Python. *Journal of Machine Learning Research*, 12(Oct):2825–2830.

Desh Peramunetilleke and R.K. Wong. 2002. Currency exchange rate forecasting from news headlines. *Australian Computer Science Communications*, 24(2):131139.

Marco Tulio Ribeiro, Sameer Singh, and Carlos Guestrin. 2016. "Why Should I Trust You?". In *Proceedings of the 22nd ACM SIGKDD International Conference on Knowledge Discovery and Data Mining - KDD '16*, pages 1135–1144, New York, New York, USA. ACM Press.

Thomas Schuster. 2003. Meta-Communication and Market Dynamics. Reflexive Interactions of Financial Markets and the Mass Media. *SSRN eLibrary*, (July).

Nitish Sinha. 2014. Using big data in finance : Example of sentiment extraction from news articles. Technical report, Board of Governors of the Federal Reserve System (US).

Carlo Strapparava and Rada Mihalcea. 2007. Semeval-2007 task 14: Affective text. *Proc. of SemEval-2007*, (June):70–74.

Eri Strumbelj, Igor Kononenko IGORKONONENKO, and Stefan Wrobel. 2010. An Efficient Explanation of Individual Classifications using Game Theory. *Journal of Machine Learning Research*, 11(Jan):1–18.

Marjan Van De Kauter, Diane Breesch, and Veronique Hoste. 2015. Fine-grained analysis of explicit and implicit sentiment in financial news articles. *Expert Systems with Applications*, 42(11):4999–5010.

Implicit and Explicit Aspect Extraction in Financial Microblogs

**Thomas Gaillat, Bernardo Stearns, Gopal Sridhar,
Ross McDermott, Manel Zarrouk**
Insight Centre for Data Analytics NUI Galway
`firstname.surname@insight-centre.org`

Brian Davis
Maynooth University
`brian.davis@mu.ie`

Abstract

This paper focuses on aspect extraction which is a sub-task of Aspect-based Sentiment Analysis. The goal is to report an extraction method of financial aspects in microblog messages. Our approach uses a stock-investment taxonomy for the identification of explicit and implicit aspects. We compare supervised and unsupervised methods to assign predefined categories at message level. Results on 7 aspect classes show 0.71 accuracy, while the 32 class classification gives 0.82 accuracy for messages containing explicit aspects and 0.35 for implicit aspects.

1 Introduction

Sentiment Analysis (SA) in the financial domain has shown a growing interest in recent years. Acquiring an insight into the public opinion of relevant and valuable economic signals can give a competitive edge and allow more informed investment decisions to be executed. Microblog platforms such as Twitter and StockTwits, are central to determining these economic signals (Bollen et al., 2011; Zhang et al., 2011). Investors share their opinions about stocks, companies and products, and these contents are valuable for whomever is interested in predicting market trends. Research in the area of SA tries to shed some light on this problem. Its purpose is to identify opinions and sentiments that are directed towards entities such as stocks and companies or towards the attributes, or aspects, of these entities.

The authors are involved in SSIX[1] (Davis et al., 2016), a project focused on SA in financial markets. It currently offers sentiment scores for stocks and companies and intends to provide finer-grained SA by including aspects. In order to conduct Aspect-Based SA in this project, the first step is to identify aspects in microblog messages, which is the focus of this paper.

As stated in SemEval-2015, the problem in Aspect-based SA can be divided into three sub-tasks, i.e. aspect category identification, Opinion Target Expression (OTE) extraction and sentiment polarity assignment (Pontiki et al., 2015). In this paper, we focus on the first sub-task of aspect category assignment. There have been two types of approaches to conduct this subtask. In the first type, aspect words are extracted and clustered (Qiu et al., 2011; Chen and Liu, 2014; Shu et al., 2016; Poria et al., 2016). In the second type, predefined aspects categories are assigned to entity-attribute pairs at sentence level (Pontiki et al., 2015). The first type of approaches targets explicit aspects while the second one also includes implicit aspects, i.e. aspects that are not explicitly mentioned in the text strings (Liu, 2012, p. 77). Using predefined aspects corresponds to the project requirements but most approaches deal with hotel, restaurant and product-related data. To the best of our knowledge none of them use a corpus of annotated aspects in the financial domain.

We present a method that focuses on the aspect category identification of implicit and explicit aspects. The originality of our work is to evaluate different aspect category identification approaches based on a predefined taxonomy of stock-investment aspects. Work is carried out on a limited data set with a view to expanding it should results be satisfactory. Our approach relies on using a corpus of annotated messages to build several types of models based on distributional semantics and supervised learning methods. Also original is that our work focuses on the stock-investment domain as it is to be added to the SSIX

---

[1] Social Sentiment IndeX is a platform dedicated to SA in financial microblogs. Available at https://ssix-project.eu/

Proceedings of the First Workshop on Economics and Natural Language Processing, pages 55–61
Melbourne, Australia, July 20, 2018. ©2018 Association for Computational Linguistics

platform. The remainder of this paper is divided as follows. Section 2 covers related work. Section 3 gives details about the corpus that was used. In Section 4 the different models are described. Results are presented in Section 5, followed by the conclusion in Section 6

2 Related Work

Available methods in aspect category identification can be divided into supervised and unsupervised approaches. Unsupervised approaches include a number of lexicon-based strategies relying on i) frequency measures used with association measures such as Point-wise Mutual Information (PMI) to link words with lexicon entries (Popescu and Etzioni, 2005; Long et al., 2010), ii) syntactic relations to relate core sentiment words, expressed by adjectives, to target aspect words expressed by nouns (Liu et al., 2016; Fang and Huang, 2012; Jo and Oh, 2011; Brody and Elhadad, 2010; Chen and Liu, 2014), and iii) on word association measures for topic extractions and clustering methods (Fang and Huang, 2012; Jo and Oh, 2011; Brody and Elhadad, 2010; Chen and Liu, 2014). All these methods rely on lexicons to search for explicit words linked to aspects.

Supervised approaches rely on Machine Learning (ML) algorithms that are trained on classified instances of aspects prior to performing classification of new instances. Many studies have proposed different types of Conditional Random Fields (CRF) models (Jakob and Gurevych, 2010; Mitchell et al., 2013; Shu et al., 2016; Cruz et al., 2014; Poria et al., 2016) that distinguish aspects from non-aspects in text sequences. In parallel, other methods apply aspect category identification on the basis of predefined aspects linked to Entity (E) and Attribute (A) pairs (Pontiki et al., 2015, 2014). The current SemEval framework requires the extraction of explicit mentions of E and of all mentions of A (implicit and explicit)(Pontiki et al., 2015).

With respect to the implicit / explicit distinction, traditional approaches have focused on explicit aspects (Liu et al., 2016; Schouten et al., 2018), hence relying on word occurrences to determine aspects. Other, more novel, methods have focused on identifying implicitly-referred-to aspects (Pontiki et al., 2015). (Dosoula et al., 2016) developed an implicit feature algorithm that uses co-occurrences to assign implicit aspects at sentence level in online restaurant reviews.

Our framework is similar to SemEval-2015 Task 12 (Pontiki et al., 2015) insofar as we used predefined categories of aspects (A) for stocks considered as entities (E). Likewise, our approach includes the extraction of aspects that are not necessarily mentioned in messages. The difference is that we use a two-level aspect taxonomy for coarse and fine-grained characterization, which gives 32 fine-grained classes as opposed to the 9 classes of the laptop data set of SE-2015 task 12 for instance. We also conduct category identification at message level without creating E/A pairs. For the requirements of the project, we use a specific financial aspect taxonomy. Albeit applied to a different domain, results show higher or equivalent F1-Scores depending on the granularity.

3 Corpus

The approach relies on a corpus of messages specialised in stock trading[2]. Microblog messages were posted by stock traders who share investment ideas and intelligence. The data set is described in Table 1.

Aspect type	Number of messages
All types	368
Implicit aspects	218
Explicit aspects	150

Table 1: Number of implicit and explicit messages in the data set

3.1 Taxonomy of Stock-Investment Aspects

As a preliminary step to aspect identification, a financial expert defined a taxonomy of trading aspects (See Appendix). They were grouped on the basis of hypo/hypernym relations following a general to more specific hierarchy. The final taxonomy consists in an aspect class dominating an aspect sub-class. No related terms, nor synonyms, were added to these subclasses. There are 7 aspect classes, e.g. *User Action, Asset Direction* and 32 aspect subclasses, e.g. *User Action>Buying Intention*. Aspect classes do not include the same number of subclasses. For instance, the *User Action* class includes 5 aspect subclasses while the *User Outlook* class includes 2 aspect subclasses. The

---

[2]The dataset is available at https://bitbucket.org/ssix-project/stock-investment-aspect-extraction

taxonomy is used i) to compute the semantic relatedness between taxonomy labels and textual candidates (DSM approach. See Section 4.1) and ii) to relate message features with taxonomy classes (Supervised-learning approach. See Section 4.2.

3.2 Annotation Scheme

The messages were manually classified by one financial expert according to the afore-mentioned taxonomy by matching aspect classes and subclasses with messages. Annotation includes the message ID and the OTE that substantiates the selected class. The following example is a JSON-type extract of the first message classified as *User Outlook > Negative Outlook*.

```
{ "ID": 1,
"AspectClass": "User Outlook",
"Aspect": "Negative Outlook",
"OTE": "Could easily see $AMZN
drop 200 points after hours
tomorrow",
"Message": "Could easily see
$AMZN drop 200 points after hours
tomorrow after earnings"
}
```

4 Building a Classification Model

This section focuses on the method used to build different models for the aspect extraction task. The task of the classifier is to assign (i) aspect classes and (ii) subclasses to messages. In this section, we present the two approaches. The first one applies a distributional semantics model, while the second one is based on several Machine Learning algorithms.

4.1 Distributional Semantics Model (DSM)

This approach relies on word embeddings for the computation of semantic relatedness with Word2vec (Mikolov et al., 2013). Word embeddings fall in the category of distributional semantics methods in which the meaning of a word is related to the distribution of words around it (Jurafsky and Martin, 2009, p.659-665).

Word2vec, in its skip-gram architecture, is such a model and was trained on the Google news corpus. The vector values are the weights computed by the hidden layer of a Neural Network trained on a corpus. The Word2vec skip-gram model allows to find words that appear frequently together, and infrequently in other contexts (Mikolov et al.

2013).

The task of identifying aspects can be formulated as mapping textual elements of messages to their most related aspect class label in the taxonomy. There are two steps: extracting candidates and computing relatedness with the classes.

4.1.1 Extracting Candidates

After preprocessing (tokenisation and Part-of-Speech (POS) tagging) The extraction of candidates relies on rule-based heuristics using morpho-syntactic patterns to select relevant Noun Phrases and Verb Phrases including modifiers such as adverbs, adjectives and present participles. The purpose is to capture fine-grained senses of these phrases. Example (1) illustrates the extraction of the item *declining revenue*.

1) $MCD with declining revenue for a good while

In example (1) only *declining revenue* is extracted. This segment is semantically relevant for the classification as *Revenue Down*, while the remainder of the NP does not procure any information regarding the type of aspect.

4.1.2 Computing Semantic Relatedness

Computing semantic relatedness consists of comparing vectors of candidates with vectors of aspect subclasses. First, multi-word candidates or labels are combined into single vectors to obtain pairs of candidate-aspect vectors. The method is the sum of the vectors of multi-word expressions. To compute relatedness between vectors, we use the Indra implementation (Freitas et al., 2016) of the cosine similarity metric. The system computes cosine similarity for all possible pairwise combinations of tokens in each message. We retain the pair with the highest score.

4.2 Supervised Learning Models

This approach relies on training several machine-learning models. Building the classifier consists in a multi-class supervised classification task.

4.2.1 Feature Engineering

After preprocessing (tokenisation, accent removal, lower-casing and POS tagging), messages were converted into vectors including the following features:

- **Bag of Words (BoW)** - They are used to create a numerical representation of the vocabulary of messages. We use three types of statistics (binary count, frequency count and tf-idf) applied on n-gram clusters.

- **Part of Speech** - PoS are used to create a numerical representation of the POS present in each message. This representation is based on the Penn Treebank POS tagset(Marcus et al., 1993).

- **Numericals** - These are used to create a representation of financial values mentioned in the messages such as percentages, ratios, stock prices and amounts (e.g. $55).

- **Predicted sentiment of entity**- The sentiment predicted[3] on the financial entities included in the messages that may contain aspects. It is a continuous value on a [-1;1] range.

4.2.2 Machine-Learning Algorithms and Optimization

A number of Machine Learning Python-based models were tested. Two methods are based on decision trees with XGboost (Chen and Guestrin, 2016) and Random Forests (Breiman, 2001). We also used Support Vector Machines (Vapnik, 2000) and Conditional Random Fields (Lafferty et al., 2001). Each of these methods use the same vector representation created in the feature engineering phase.

In order to find the best hyper-parameters for the tested models, we used the Particle Swarm Optimization (PSO) method. This method was appropriate due to the fact that hyper-parameters are numbers, mostly in a continuous space. PSO (Kennedy and Eberhart, 1995) was applied using 100 particles (specific hyper-parameter configurations) during 100 iterations, using same weights for velocity, particle best and global best. For each particle position, the average accuracy in 10-fold cross validation was calculated.

4.3 Model Selection, Validation and Evaluation

Choosing the best classifier is done in two stages. Firstly, a model selection procedure helps select the best model among the DSM and ML models. All models were tested with 10-fold cross-validation whereby the dataset is divided in ten parts. Each part is used as a test set once in the ten

---

[3]with the use of the SSIX FinSentiA Sentiment Analyser (Gaillat et al., 2018).

iterations of the process. Secondly, the selected model is validated by using the leave-one-out option, meaning that the training is conducted on all instances except one. The process is repeated until all instances have been used as a test instance.

In the model selection stage we computed global accuracy for 32 classes. In the validation stage, we used F1-Score for 7 and 32 classes to measure the effects of the coarse and fine-grained annotation levels. The annotated corpus described in Section 3 was used for training and testing. In the DSM approach, 172 initially annotated messages were used as test set.

5 Results and Discussion

In the model selection stage all of the approaches show different results as shown in Table 2.

Model	Accuracy	Standard deviation
DSM (baseline)	0.425	-
ML Methods		
Xgboost	0.5689	0.046
Random Forest	0.5435	0.038
SVC	0.449	0.027
CRF	0.431	0.052

Table 2: Model selection stage: Accuracy for each model for the 32 aspect classification task

Xgboost was selected and validation showed results (see Table 3) in line with the best scores obtained in SemEval-2015 Task 12.

Table 4 shows the accuracy for message classification according to the implicit or explicit nature of the 32 aspects. The distinction between implicit and explicit aspect messages shows that explicit aspects are well classified while implicit aspects are only correctly handled in about 35% of cases. This suggests that the classifier lacks significant features to identify implicit aspects. The size of the data set appears to be a limitation but the size of sentences may also impair the classifier by adding noise to the data. Using aspect-relevant OTEs as a BoW feature could help address this point.

6 Conclusion and Future Work

In this paper, we have reported on a series of experiments in the domain of Aspect Extraction. The experiments focused on the sub-task of aspect cat-

Model	Acc	F1-Score	P	R
Xgboost (32 classes)	0.565	0.49	0.52	0.49
Xgboost (7 classes)	0.712	0.71	0.70	0.71

Table 3: Model validation stage: Accuracy, F1-Score, Precision (P) and Recall (R) for the 32 and 7 aspect classification task

Aspects	Acc	F1-Score	P	R
Implicit	0.351	0.32	0.28	0.28
Explicit	0.826	0.8	0.84	0.8

Table 4: Accuracy according to messages including 32 implicit and explicit aspects

egory identification in the domain of stock investments. A taxonomy was used to identify predefined aspects in microblog messages. A distributional semantics model and several supervised learning methods were used for the task.

Results show that explicit aspect identification performs well, but implicit aspect identification remains an issue that can be tackled with larger data set and improved feature engineering. Despite the size of the training data set, results suggest that more efforts can be invested in the development of a larger data set.

7 Appendix

Taxonomy of stock-investment aspects

- User Action
    - Buying Intention
    - Selling Intention
    - Bought
    - Sold
    - Shorting
- User Outlook
    - Positive Outlook
    - Negative Outlook
- Insider Activity
    - Insider Selling
    - Insider Buying
- Asset Direction
    - Moving Higher
    - Moving Lower
    - Breakout
    - New High
    - Trending Higher
    - Trending Lower
    - Trending Sideways
- Asset Behaviour
    - Oversold
    - Overbought
    - Overvalued
    - Undervalued
    - Short Squeeze
    - Selling Pressure
- Financial Results
    - Earnings Beat
    - Earnings Miss
    - Revenue Up
    - Revenue Down
    - Profit Warning
- Analyst Ratings
    - Buy Recommendation
    - Sell Recommendation
    - Rating Upgrade
    - Rating Downgrade

References

Johan Bollen, Huina Mao, and Xiao-Jun Zeng. 2011. Twitter mood predicts the stock market. *Journal of Computational Science*, 2(1):1–8.

Leo Breiman. 2001. Random Forests. *Machine Learning*, 45(1):5–32.

Samuel Brody and Noemie Elhadad. 2010. An Unsupervised Aspect-sentiment Model for Online Reviews. In *Human Language Technologies: The 2010 Annual Conference of the North American Chapter of the Association for Computational Linguistics*, HLT '10, pages 804–812, Stroudsburg, PA, USA. Association for Computational Linguistics.

Tianqi Chen and Carlos Guestrin. 2016. XGBoost: A Scalable Tree Boosting System. In *Proceedings of the 22Nd ACM SIGKDD International Conference on Knowledge Discovery and Data Mining*, KDD '16, pages 785–794, New York, NY, USA. ACM.

Zhiyuan Chen and Bing Liu. 2014. Topic Modeling Using Topics from Many Domains, Lifelong Learning and Big Data. In *Proceedings of the 31st International Conference on International Conference on Machine Learning - Volume 32*, ICML'14, pages II–703–II–711, Beijing, China. JMLR.org.

Ivan Cruz, Alexander F. Gelbukh, and Grigori Sidorov. 2014. Implicit Aspect Indicator Extraction for Aspect based Opinion Mining. *Int. J. Comput. Linguistics Appl.*, 5:135–152.

Brian Davis, Keith Cortis, Laurentiu Vasiliu, Adamantios Koumpis, Ross Mcdermott, and Siegfried Handschuh. 2016. Social Sentiment Indices Powered by X-Scores. In *ALLDATA 2016 , The Second International Conference on Big Data, Small Data, Linked Data and Open Data*, Lisbon, Portugal. International Academy, Research, and Industry Association (IARIA).

Nikoleta Dosoula, Roel Griep, Rick den Ridder, Rick Slangen, Ruud van Luijk, Kim Schouten, and Flavius Frasincar. 2016. Sentiment Analysis of Multiple Implicit Features per Sentence in Consumer Review Data. In *Databases and Information Systems (DB&IS)*, Riga, Latvia. Springer.

Lei Fang and Minlie Huang. 2012. Fine Granular Aspect Analysis Using Latent Structural Models. In *Proceedings of the 50th Annual Meeting of the Association for Computational Linguistics: Short Papers - Volume 2*, ACL '12, pages 333–337, Stroudsburg, PA, USA. Association for Computational Linguistics.

André Freitas, Siamak Barzegar, Juliano Efson Sales, Siegfried Handschuh, and Brian Davis. 2016. Semantic Relatedness for All (Languages): A Comparative Analysis of Multilingual Semantic Relatedness Using Machine Translation. In Eva Blomqvist, Paolo Ciancarini, Francesco Poggi, and Fabio Vitali, editors, *Knowledge Engineering and Knowledge Management: 20th International Conference, EKAW 2016, Bologna, Italy, November 19-23, 2016, Proceedings*, pages 212–222. Springer International Publishing, Cham.

Thomas Gaillat, Annanda Sousa, Manel Zarrouk, and Brian, Davis. 2018. FinSentiA: Sentiment Analysis in English Financial Microblogs. In *Proceedings of the TALN-CORIA 2018*, Rennes, France. Revue TAL.

Niklas Jakob and Iryna Gurevych. 2010. Extracting Opinion Targets in a Single- and Cross-domain Setting with Conditional Random Fields. In *Proceedings of the 2010 Conference on Empirical Methods in Natural Language Processing*, EMNLP '10, pages 1035–1045, Stroudsburg, PA, USA. Association for Computational Linguistics.

Yohan Jo and Alice H. Oh. 2011. Aspect and Sentiment Unification Model for Online Review Analysis. In *Proceedings of the Fourth ACM International Conference on Web Search and Data Mining*, WSDM '11, pages 815–824, New York, NY, USA. ACM.

Daniel Jurafsky and James H. Martin. 2009. *Speech and Language Processing (2nd Edition)*. Prentice-Hall, Inc., Upper Saddle River, NJ, USA.

James Kennedy and Russel Eberhart. 1995. Particle swarm optimization. In , *IEEE International Conference on Neural Networks, 1995. Proceedings*, volume 4, pages 1942–1948 vol.4.

John D. Lafferty, Andrew McCallum, and Fernando C. N. Pereira. 2001. Conditional Random Fields: Probabilistic Models for Segmenting and Labeling Sequence Data. In *Proceedings of the Eighteenth International Conference on Machine Learning*, ICML '01, pages 282–289, San Francisco, CA, USA. Morgan Kaufmann Publishers Inc.

Bing Liu. 2012. *Sentiment Analysis and Opinion Mining*. Morgan & Claypool Publishers, San Rafael, Calif.

Qian Liu, Bing Liu, Yuanlin Zhang, Doo Soon Kim, and Zhiqiang Gao. 2016. Improving Opinion Aspect Extraction Using Semantic Similarity and Aspect Associations. In *Thirtieth AAAI Conference on Artificial Intelligence*, Phoenix, Arizona USA. AAAI Press.

Chong Long, Jie Zhang, and Xiaoyan Zhu. 2010. A Review Selection Approach for Accurate Feature Rating Estimation. In *Proceedings of the 23rd International Conference on Computational Linguistics: Posters*, COLING '10, pages 766–774, Stroudsburg, PA, USA. Association for Computational Linguistics.

Mitchell P. Marcus, Mary Ann Marcinkiewicz, and Beatrice Santorini. 1993. Building a Large Annotated Corpus of English: The Penn Treebank. *Computational Linguistics*, 19(2):313–330.

Tomas Mikolov, Kai Chen, Greg Corrado, and Jeffrey Dean. 2013. Efficient Estimation of Word Representations in Vector Space. ArXiv: 1301.3781.

Margaret Mitchell, Jacqueline Aguilar, Theresa Wilson, and Benjamin Van Durme. 2013. Open Domain Targeted Sentiment. In *Proceedings of the 2013 Conference on Empirical Methods in Natural Language Processing*, pages 1643–1654, Seattle, Washington, USA. ACL.

Maria Pontiki, Dimitris Galanis, Haris Papageorgiou, Suresh Manandhar, and Ion Androutsopoulos. 2015. SemEval-2015 Task 12: Aspect Based Sentiment Analysis. In *Proceedings of the 9th International Workshop on Semantic Evaluation (SemEval 2015)*, pages 486–495, Denver, USA. The Association for Computational Linguistics.

Maria Pontiki, Dimitris Galanis, John Pavlopoulos, Harris Papageorgiou, Ion Androutsopoulos, and Suresh Manandhar. 2014. SemEval-2014 Task 4:

Aspect Based Sentiment Analysis. In *Proceedings of the 8th International Workshop on Semantic Evaluation (SemEval 2014)*, pages 27–35, Dublin, Ireland. Association for Computational Linguistics and Dublin City University.

Ana-Maria Popescu and Oren Etzioni. 2005. Extracting Product Features and Opinions from Reviews. In *Proceedings of the Conference on Human Language Technology and Empirical Methods in Natural Language Processing*, HLT '05, pages 339–346, Stroudsburg, PA, USA. Association for Computational Linguistics.

Soujanya Poria, Erik Cambria, and Alexander Gelbukh. 2016. Aspect extraction for opinion mining with a deep convolutional neural network. *Knowledge-Based Systems*, 108(Supplement C):42–49.

Guang Qiu, Bing Liu, Jiajun Bu, and Chun Chen. 2011. Opinion Word Expansion and Target Extraction Through Double Propagation. *Comput. Linguist.*, 37(1):9–27.

K. Schouten, O. van der Weijde, F. Frasincar, and R. Dekker. 2018. Supervised and Unsupervised Aspect Category Detection for Sentiment Analysis with Co-occurrence Data. *IEEE Transactions on Cybernetics*, 48(4):1263–1275.

Lei Shu, Bing Liu, Hu Xu, and Annice Kim. 2016. Supervised Opinion Aspect Extraction by Exploiting Past Extraction Results. *CoRR*, abs/1612.07940.

Vladimir Vapnik. 2000. *The Nature of Statistical Learning Theory*, 2 edition. Information Science and Statistics. Springer-Verlag, New York.

Xue Zhang, Hauke Fuehres, and Peter A. Gloor. 2011. Predicting Stock Market Indicators Through Twitter I hope it is not as bad as I fear. *Procedia - Social and Behavioral Sciences*, 26(Supplement C):55–62.

Unsupervised Word Influencer Networks from News Streams

Ananth Balashankar
New York University
ananth@nyu.edu

Sunandan Chakraborty
Indiana University
sunchak@iu.edu

Lakshminarayanan Subramanian
New York University
lakshmi@cs.nyu.edu

Abstract

In this paper, we propose a new unsupervised learning framework to use news events for predicting trends in stock prices. We present *Word Influencer Networks (WIN)*, a graph framework to extract longitudinal temporal relationships between any pair of informative words from news streams. Using the temporal occurrence of words, WIN measures how the appearance of one word in a news stream *influences* the emergence of another set of words in the future. The latent word-word influencer relationships in WIN are the building blocks for causal reasoning and predictive modeling. We demonstrate the efficacy of WIN by using it for unsupervised extraction of latent features for stock price prediction and obtain 2 orders lower prediction error compared to a similar causal graph based method. WIN discovered influencer links from seemingly unrelated words from topics like politics to finance. WIN also validated 67% of the causal evidence found manually in the text through a direct edge and the rest 33% through a path of length 2.

1 Introduction

Stock price prediction using financial news events and social media sentiments have been studied extensively in literature. Most of these works rely on extracting rich features from relevant financial news of companies (Falinouss, 2007; Kalyani et al., 2016; Hagenau et al., 2013; Shynkevich et al., 2015), Twitter sentiments of financial terms (Mao et al., 2011; Rao and Srivastava, 2012; Bernardo et al., 2018) and market volatility measures (Balcilar et al., 2017; Sun et al., 2014) as

features to predict trends in their stock prices. However, none of these approaches tried to exploit *unknown* or *little known* relationships between news events and stock prices. Previous works used "known" factors and used them as features to predict stock prices by extracting them from news stories. There might be other unknown (and non-finance related) factors potentially influencing stock prices that cannot be discovered using these methods.

This paper aims to understand unknown and latent relationships between words that describe events in news streams to potentially uncover *hidden* links between news events and apply those *new* relationships to build a news-driven predictive model for stock prices. The appearance of these relationship entities in news, may be well separated over time. For example, market volatility is known to be triggered by recessions; this hidden relationship may manifest in new streams with a frequency spike in the word "recession" followed by a frequency spike in the word "volatility", a *few weeks later*. Thus, mining large news datasets can potentially reveal influencing factors behind the surge of a particular word in news. This notion can be generalized to discover the influence of one event to another, where the events are manifested by specific words appearing in news.

In this paper, we propose a new framework – *Word Influencer Networks (WIN)* that aims at detecting the latent relationships between words, where such relationships are not directly observed. WIN differs from existing relationship extraction and representational frameworks across two dimensions – (1) unsupervised causal relationships instead of associative ones that can be used to understand a path of *influence* among news items, (2) finding inter-topic influence relationships outside the "context" or the confines of a single document. Construction of WIN can be used to build

Proceedings of the First Workshop on Economics and Natural Language Processing, pages 62–68
Melbourne, Australia, July 20, 2018. ©2018 Association for Computational Linguistics

predictive models for numerous *news-dependent* variables, including stock prices.

We constructed WIN from a news corpus of around $700,000$ articles and evaluated it to extract features for stock price prediction and obtained two orders lower prediction error compared to a similar causal graph based method. WIN also validated 67% of the causal evidence found manually in the text through a direct edge in the network and the rest through a path of length 2. We also evaluated the network qualitatively for sparsity and its capacity to generate "out of context" inter-topic word relationships on the entire vocabulary.

2 Related Work

Online news articles are a popular source for mining real-world events, including extraction of causal relationships. Radinsky and Horvitz (Radinsky and Horvitz, 2013) proposed a framework to find causal relationships between events to predict future events from News but caters to a small number of events. Causal relationships extracted from news using Granger causality have also been used for predicting variables, such as stock prices (Kang et al., 2017; Verma et al., 2017; Darrat et al., 2007). A similar causal relationship generation model has been proposed by Hashimoto et al. (2015) to extract causal relationships from natural language text. A similar approach can be observed in (Kozareva, 2012; Do et al., 2011), whereas CATENA system (Mirza and Tonelli, 2016) used a hybrid approach consisting of a rule-based component and a supervised classifier. WIN differs from these approaches as it explores latent inter-topic causal relationships in an unsupervised manner from the entire vocabulary of words and collocated N-grams.

Apart from using causality, there are many other methods explored to extract information from news and are used in time series based forecasting. Amodeo et al. (Amodeo et al., 2011) proposed a hybrid model consisting of time-series analysis, to predict future events using the New York Times corpus. FBLG (Cheng et al., 2014) focused on discovering temporal dependency from time series data and applied it to a Twitter dataset mentioning the Haiti earthquake. Similar work by Luo et al. (Luo et al., 2014) showed correlations between real-world events and time-series data for incident diagnosis in online services. Other similar works like, Trend Analysis Model (TAM) (Kawa-

mae, 2011) and Temporal-LDA (TM-LDA) (Wang et al., 2012) model the temporal aspect of topics in social media streams like Twitter. Structured data extraction from news have also been used for stock price prediction using techniques of information retrieval in (Ding et al., 2014; Xie et al., 2013; Ding et al., 2015; Chang et al., 2016; Ding et al., 2016). Vaca et al. (Vaca et al., 2014) used a collective matrix factorization method to track emerging, fading and evolving topics in news streams. WIN is inspired by such time series models and leverages the Granger causality detection framework for the trend prediction task.

3 Word Influence Network

Word Influence Network (WIN) addresses the discovery of *influence* between words that appear in news text. The identification of influence link between words is based on temporal co-variance, so that answers to questions of the form "Does the appearance of word x influence the appearance of word y after δ days?" can be addressed. The influence of one word on another is determined based on pairwise causal relationships and is computed using Granger causality test. Following the identification of Granger causal pairs of words, such pairs are combined together to form a network of words, where the directed edges depict potential influence between words. The network provides a more holistic view of the causal information flow by overcoming a common drawback of pair-wise Granger causality, when the true relationship involves three or more variables (Maziarz, 2015). In the final network an edge or a path between a word pair represents a flow of influence from the source word to the final word and this *influence* depicts an increase in the appearance of the final words when the source word was observed in news data.

The word influencer network can offer the following that can significantly increase the benefits of using news for analytics – (1) Detection of influence path, (2) Discovery of unknown facts, (3) Hypothesis testing and (4) Feature extraction for experiment design.

4 Methodology

Construction of WIN from the raw unstructured news data, finding pairwise causal links and eventually building the influence network involves numerous challenges. In the rest of the section we discuss the design methodologies used to overcome these challenges along with some properties of the network.

Selecting *Informative* Words: Only a small percentage of the words appearing in news can be used for meaningful information extraction and analysis. There are some words that are *too frequent* and some are *too rare* to establish any significant relationship(Manning et al., 1999; Hovold, 2005). Any word whose frequencies were in those range were removed. Specifically, we eliminated too frequent (at least once in more than 50% of the days) or too rare (appearing in less than 100 articles). These thresholds were determined empirically by looking at the temporal frequency distribution of the words. Many common English nouns, adjectives and verbs, whose contribution to semantics is minimal(Forman, 2003) carry very little significance were also removed from the vocabulary. However, named-entities were retained for their newsworthiness and a set of trigger words were retained that depicts events (e.g. flood, election) using an existing event trigger detection algorithm. The vocabulary set was enhanced by adding bigrams that are significantly collocated in the corpus, such as, 'fuel price' and 'prime minister' etc. after applying similar filtering methods as described for words.

Time-series Representation of News Data: Consider a corpus $\mathcal{D}$ of news articles indexed by time t, such that $\mathcal{D}_t$ is the collection of news articles published at time t. Each article $d \in D$ is a collection of words W_d, where i^{th} word $w_{d,i} \in W_d$ is drawn from a vocabulary V of size N. The set of articles published at time t can be expressed in terms of the words appearing in the articles as $\{\alpha_1^t, \alpha_2^t, ..., \alpha_N^t\}$, where α_i^t is the sum of frequency of the word $w_i \in V$ across all articles published at time t. α_i^t corresponding to $w_i \in V$ is defined as, $\alpha_i^t = \frac{\mu_i^t}{\sum_{t=1}^{T} \mu_i^t}$ where $\mu_i^t = \sum_{d=1}^{|D_t|} TF(w_{d,i})$. α_i^t is normalized by using the frequency distribution of w_i in the entire time period. $\mathcal{T}(w_i)$ represents the time series of the word w_i, where i varies from 1 to N, the vocabulary size.

4.1 Measuring Influence between Words

Given two time-series X and Y, the Granger causality test checks whether the X is more effective in predicting Y than using just Y and if this holds then the test concludes X "Granger-causes" Y (Granger et al., 2000). However, if both X and Y are driven by a common third process with different lags, one might still fail to reject the alternative hypothesis of Granger causality. Hence, in WIN, we explore the possibility of causal links between all word pairs and detect triangulated relations to eliminate the risk of ignoring confounding variables, otherwise not considered in Granger causality test.

Constructing WIN using an exhaustive set of word pairs can be computationally challenging and prohibitively expensive when the vocabulary size is fairly large. This is true in our case, where even after using a reduced set of words and including the collocated phrases, the vocabulary size is around $39,000$. One solution to this problem is considering the Lasso Granger method (Arnold et al., 2007) that applies regression to the neighborhood selection problem for any word, given the fact that the best regressor for that variable with the least squared error will have non-zero coefficients only for the lagged variables in the neighborhood. The Lasso algorithm for linear regression is an incremental algorithm that embodies a method of variable selection (Tibshirani, 1994). In our case, if we are determining the influence link between a word y to the rest, then,

$$\mathbf{w} = argmin \frac{1}{N} \Sigma_{(\mathbf{x},y) \in V} |\mathbf{w}.\mathbf{x} - y|^2 + \lambda ||\mathbf{w}|| \quad (1)$$

where V is the input vocabulary from the news dataset, N is the vocabulary size, x is the list of all lagged variables (maximum lag of 30 days per word) of the vocabulary and λ is a constant to be determined. To set λ, we use the method used in (Meinshausen and Bühlmann, 2006). We select the variables that have non-zero co-efficients and choose the best lag for a given variable based on the maximum absolute value of a word's coefficient. We then, draw an edge from all these words to the predicted word with the annotations of the optimal time lag (in days) and incrementally construct the graph as illustrated in Figure 3.

4.2 Topic Influence Compression

The number of nodes in this version of WIN corresponds to the vocabulary size and it can be hard to visualize the graph due to its size. To make information gathering from WIN easier, we make the graph coarser by clustering the nodes based on *topics*. Topics are learned from the original news corpus using Latent Dirichlet Allocation (LDA)(Blei et al., 2003). Influence is generalized to topic level by calculating the weight of inter-topic influence relationships as a total number of edges between vertices of two topics. The strength of this influence is defined as,

$$\Phi(\theta_u, \theta_v) = \frac{\#\ \text{Edges between u and v}}{(|\theta_u| \times |\theta_v|)} \qquad (2)$$

where, θ_u and θ_v are two topics in our topic model and $|\theta_u|$ represents the size of topic θ_u, i.e. the number of words in the topic whose topic-probability is greater than 0.001. $\Phi(\theta_u, \theta_v)$ is termed as *strong* if its value is within the top 1% of Φ for all topics. Any edge in the original WIN is removed if there are no strong topic edges between the corresponding word nodes. This filtered topic graph has only edges between topics which have high influence strength.

5 Evaluation

5.1 Data

The news dataset[1] we used for stock price prediction contains news crawled from 2010 to 2013 using Google News APIs and New York Times data from 1989 to 2007. We construct WIN from the time series representation of its 12,804 unigrams and 25,909 bigrams, as well as the 10 stock prices[2] from 2013 we use for prediction. The prediction is done with varying step sizes (1,3,5), which indicates the time lag between the news data and the day of the predicted stock price in days. In order to qualitatively validate that latent inter-topic edges exist in the news stream, we also constructed WIN from the online archives of Times of India (TOI), the most circulated Indian English newspaper. This dataset contains all the articles published in their online edition between January 1, 2006 and December 31, 2015 containing 1,538,932 articles.

5.2 Inter-topic edges of WIN

The influence network we constructed from the TOI dataset has 18,541 edges and 7,190 unigrams and bi-gram vertices. We split the edges to inter-topic (9774) edges and intra-topic (8765) edges. We were interested in the inter-topic non-associative relationships that WIN is expected to capture. From Figure 1, we can see many topics (44) do not have inter-topic influence relationships, but a few topics (5) influence or are influenced by a large number of topics. Some of these

highly influential topics are composed of words describing "Education", "Economics", "Politics", "Crime" and "Agriculture", and the maximum number of influencer relationships in WIN is from "Politics" to "Crime".

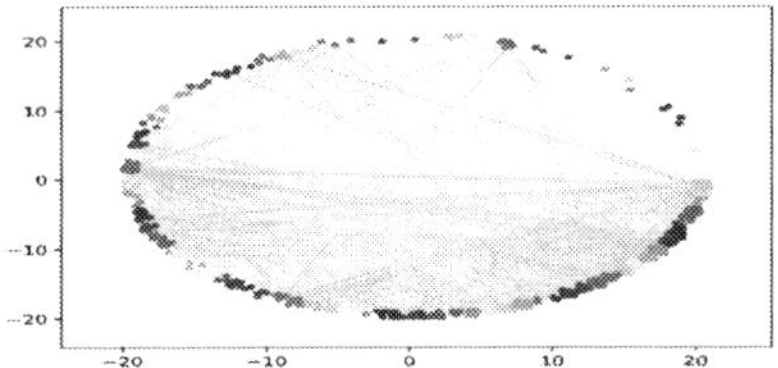

Figure 1: Inter-topic word relationships

5.2.1 Links of the network

Inspecting the links and paths of WIN gives us qualitative insights into the context in which the word-word relationships were established. Since WIN is also capable of representing other stock time series as potential influencers in the network, we can use this to model the propagation of shocks in the market as shown in Figure 2. WIN also highlights one of the limitations of granger causality by running on the entire vocabulary as shown in Figure 3, i.e if an underlying event (slum rehabilitation) causes two other events at different time lags (provided relief and coordinate committee), the link between the two lagged events can be pruned as it is dependent on the underlying cause.

5.3 Prediction using causal links

To evaluate the causal links generated by WIN, we use it to extract features for predicting stock prices using the exact data and prediction setting used in Kang et al. (2017). Note that the features and topics were not chosen in an unsupervised manner in Kang et al. (2017), but rather based on a semantic parser. Once the features are extracted from WIN, we use the past values of stock prices and time series corresponding to the incoming word edges of WIN to predict the future values

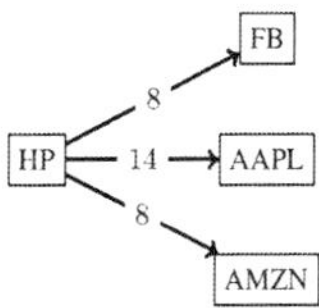

Figure 2: Inter-stock influencer links

[1] https://github.com/dykang/cgraph
[2] https://finance.yahoo.com

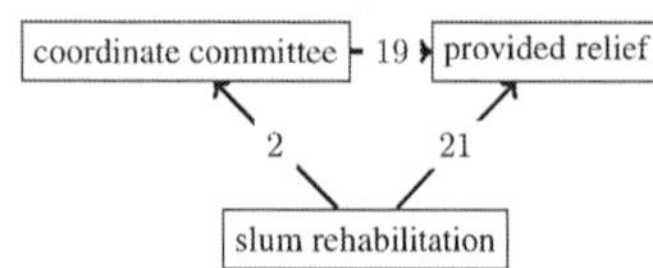

Figure 3: WIN highlighting the underlying cause

Table 1: Stock price prediction error using WIN

Step size	C_{best}	WIN_{uni}	WIN_{bi}	WIN_{both}
1	1.96	0.022	0.023	0.020
3	3.78	0.022	0.023	0.022
5	5.25	0.022	0.023	0.021

of the stock prices using the multivariate regression equation used to determine Granger Causality. The results shown in Table 1 is the root mean squared error (RMSE) calculated on a 30 day window averaged by moving it by 10 days over the period and hence is directly comparable to (Kang et al., 2017)'s CGRAPH - C_{best}. The mean absolute error (MAE) for the same set of evaluations is within 0.003 of the RMSE, which indicates that the variance of the errors is also low. As compared to their best error, WIN from unigrams, bigrams or both obtain two orders lower error and significantly outperforms CGRAPH, which also includes features from topics and sentiments from tweets. We attribute this gain to the flexibility of WIN's Lasso Granger method to produce sparse graphs as compared to CGRAPH's Vector Auto Regressive model with exogenous variables which uses a fixed number (10) of incoming edges per node. This imposes an artificial bound on sparsity thereby losing valuable information. We overcome this in WIN using a suitable penalty term (λ) in the Lasso method.

The causal links in WIN are also more generic (Table 2) than the ones described in CGRAPH. The nodes of CGRAPH are tuples extracted from a semantic parser (SEMAFOR) based on evidence of causality in a sentence. WIN poses no such restriction and and derives topical (unfriended, FB) and inter-topical (healthcare, AMZN), sparse, latent and semantic relationships.

5.4 Causal evidence in WIN

To validate the causal links in WIN, we extracted word pairs which depicted direct causal relationships in the news corpus. We narrowed down the search to words surrounding verbs which depict the notion of causality like "caused", "effect" and

Table 2: Stock price predictive features from WIN

Stock symbol	Prediction indicators
AAPL	workplace, shutter, music
AMZN	healthcare, HBO, cloud
FB	unfriended, troll, politician
GOOG	advertisers, artificial intelligence, shake-up
HPQ	China, inventions, Pittsburg
IBM	64 GB, redesign, outage
MSFT	interactive, security, Broadcom
ORCL	corporate, investing, multimedia
TSLA	prices, testers, controversy
YHOO	entertainment, leadership, investment

manually verified that these word pairs were indeed causal. We then searched the shortest path in WIN between these word pairs. 67% of the word pairs which were manually identified to be causal in the news text through causal indicator words such as "caused", were linked in WIN through direct edges, while the rest were linked through an intermediate relevant node. As seen in Table 3, the bigram involving the word in the path is relevant to the context in which the causality is established. The time lags in the path show that the influence between events are at different time lags. We also qualitatively verified that two unrelated words are either not connected or have a path length greater than 2, which makes the relationship weak.

Table 3: Comparison with manually identified influence from news articles

Word pairs	Words of the influence path
price, project	price-hike –(19)– power-project
land, budget	allot-land –(22)– railway-budget
price, land	price-hike –(12)– land
strike, law	terror-strike –(25)– law ministry
land, bill	land-reform –(25)– bill-pass

6 Conclusions

In this paper, we have presented WIN, a framework that learns latent word relationships from news streams in an unsupervised manner for stock price prediction. This prediction model considerably lowers the error as compared to a related causal graph method by capturing rich inter-topical features. In future work, we aim to extend the concept of *influencer network* for other types of text abstraction, like word embeddings and explore influencer network based econometric predictive models.

References

Giuseppe Amodeo, Roi Blanco, and Ulf Brefeld. 2011. Hybrid models for future event prediction. CIKM '11, pages 1981–1984.

Andrew Arnold, Yan Liu, and Naoki Abe. 2007. Temporal causal modeling with graphical granger methods. In *Proceedings of the 13th ACM SIGKDD International Conference on Knowledge Discovery and Data Mining*, KDD '07, pages 66–75, New York, NY, USA. ACM.

Mehmet Balcilar, Rangan Gupta, and Clement Kyei. 2017. Predicting stock returns and volatility with investor sentiment indices: A reconsideration using a nonparametric causalityinquantiles test. *Bulletin of Economic Research*, 70(1):74–87.

Ivo Bernardo, Roberto Henriques, and Victor Lobo. 2018. Social market: Stock market and twitter correlation. In *Intelligent Decision Technologies 2017*, pages 341–356, Cham. Springer International Publishing.

David M. Blei, Andrew Y. Ng, and Michael I. Jordan. 2003. Latent dirichlet allocation. *J. Mach. Learn. Res.*, 3:993–1022.

Ching-Yun Chang, Yue Zhang, Zhiyang Teng, Zahn Bozanic, and Bin Ke. 2016. Measuring the information content of financial news. In *COLING*, pages 3216–3225. ACL.

Dehua Cheng, Mohammad Taha Bahadori, and Yan Liu. 2014. Fblg: A simple and effective approach for temporal dependence discovery from time series data. KDD '14, pages 382–391.

Ali F. Darrat, Maosen Zhong, and Louis T.W. Cheng. 2007. Intraday volume and volatility relations with and without public news. *Journal of Banking and Finance*, 31(9):2711 – 2729.

Xiao Ding, Yue Zhang, Ting Liu, and Junwen Duan. 2014. Using structured events to predict stock price movement: An empirical investigation.

Xiao Ding, Yue Zhang, Ting Liu, and Junwen Duan. 2015. Deep learning for event-driven stock prediction. In *IJCAI*, pages 2327–2333. AAAI Press.

Xiao Ding, Yue Zhang, Ting Liu, and Junwen Duan. 2016. Knowledge-driven event embedding for stock prediction. In *COLING*, pages 2133–2142. ACL.

Quang Xuan Do, Yee Seng Chan, and Dan Roth. 2011. Minimally supervised event causality identification. In *Proceedings of the Conference on Empirical Methods in Natural Language Processing*, EMNLP '11, pages 294–303, Stroudsburg, PA, USA. Association for Computational Linguistics.

Pegah Falinouss. 2007. Stock trend prediction using news events. *Masters thesis*.

George Forman. 2003. An extensive empirical study of feature selection metrics for text classification. *Journal of machine learning research*, 3(Mar):1289–1305.

Clive WJ Granger, Bwo-Nung Huangb, and Chin-Wei Yang. 2000. A bivariate causality between stock prices and exchange rates: evidence from recent asianflu. *The Quarterly Review of Economics and Finance*, 40(3):337–354.

Michael Hagenau, Michael Liebmann, and Dirk Neumann. 2013. Automated news reading: Stock price prediction based on financial news using context-capturing features. *Decision Support Systems*, 55(3):685 – 697.

Chikara Hashimoto, Kentaro Torisawa, Julien Kloetzer, and Jong-Hoon Oh. 2015. Generating event causality hypotheses through semantic relations. In *Proceedings of the Twenty-Ninth AAAI Conference on Artificial Intelligence*, AAAI'15, pages 2396–2403. AAAI Press.

Johan Hovold. 2005. Naive bayes spam filtering using word-position-based attributes. In *CEAS*, pages 41–48.

Joshi Kalyani, H. N. Bharathi, and Rao Jyothi. 2016. Stock trend prediction using news sentiment analysis. *CoRR*, abs/1607.01958.

Dongyeop Kang, Varun Gangal, Ang Lu, Zheng Chen, and Eduard Hovy. 2017. Detecting and explaining causes from text for a time series event. In *Proceedings of the 2017 Conference on Empirical Methods in Natural Language Processing*, pages 2758–2767, Copenhagen, Denmark. Association for Computational Linguistics.

Noriaki Kawamae. 2011. Trend analysis model: trend consists of temporal words, topics, and timestamps. WSDM '11, pages 317–326.

Zornitsa Kozareva. 2012. Cause-effect relation learning. In *Workshop Proceedings of TextGraphs-7 on Graph-based Methods for Natural Language Processing*, TextGraphs-7 '12, pages 39–43, Stroudsburg, PA, USA. Association for Computational Linguistics.

Chen Luo, Jian-Guang Lou, Qingwei Lin, Qiang Fu, Rui Ding, Dongmei Zhang, and Zhe Wang. 2014. Correlating events with time series for incident diagnosis. KDD '14, pages 1583–1592.

Christopher D Manning, Hinrich Schütze, et al. 1999. *Foundations of statistical natural language processing*, volume 999. MIT Press.

Huina Mao, Scott Counts, and Johan Bollen. 2011. Predicting financial markets: Comparing survey, news, twitter and search engine data. *Arxiv preprint*.

Mariusz Maziarz. 2015. A review of the granger-causality fallacy. *The Journal of Philosophical Economics*, 8(2):6.

Nicolai Meinshausen and Peter Bühlmann. 2006. High-dimensional graphs and variable selection with the lasso. *The annals of statistics*, pages 1436–1462.

Paramita Mirza and Sara Tonelli. 2016. Catena: Causal and temporal relation extraction from natural language texts. In *Proceedings of COLING 2016, the 26th International Conference on Computational Linguistics: Technical Papers*, pages 64–75. The COLING 2016 Organizing Committee.

Kira Radinsky and Eric Horvitz. 2013. Mining the web to predict future events. WSDM '13, pages 255–264. ACM.

Tushar Rao and Saket Srivastava. 2012. Analyzing stock market movements using twitter sentiment analysis. In *Proceedings of the 2012 International Conference on Advances in Social Networks Analysis and Mining (ASONAM 2012)*, ASONAM '12, pages 119–123, Washington, DC, USA. IEEE Computer Society.

Y. Shynkevich, T. M. McGinnity, S. Coleman, and A. Belatreche. 2015. Stock price prediction based on stock-specific and sub-industry-specific news articles. In *2015 International Joint Conference on Neural Networks (IJCNN)*, pages 1–8.

X-Q Sun, Shen H-W, and Cheng X-Q. 2014. Trading network predicts stock price. *Scientific Reports. 2014;4:3711. doi:10.1038/srep03711.*

Robert Tibshirani. 1994. Regression shrinkage and selection via the lasso. *Journal of the Royal Statistical Society, Series B*, 58:267–288.

Carmen K Vaca, Amin Mantrach, Alejandro Jaimes, and Marco Saerens. 2014. A time-based collective factorization for topic discovery and monitoring in news. WWW '14, pages 527–538.

Ishan Verma, Lipika Dey, and Hardik Meisheri. 2017. Detecting, quantifying and accessing impact of news events on indian stock indices. In *Proceedings of the International Conference on Web Intelligence*, WI '17, pages 550–557, New York, NY, USA. ACM.

Yu Wang, Eugene Agichtein, and Michele Benzi. 2012. Tm-lda: efficient online modeling of latent topic transitions in social media. KDD '12, pages 123–131. ACM.

Boyi Xie, Rebecca J. Passonneau, Leon Wu, and Germán Creamer. 2013. Semantic frames to predict stock price movement. In *ACL (1)*, pages 873–883. The Association for Computer Linguistics.